T

SOLD
ON PUR
POSE

MARKETING **TO THE CONSCIOUS** CONSUMER

Editor: Karen Rowe, www.karenrowe.com

Cover Design: Shake Creative, ShakeTampa.com

Inside Layout: Ljiljana Pavkov

Printed in the United States

ISBN: 978-0-578-47217-1 (paperback)

ISBN: 978-0-578-47218-8 (ebook)

ISBN: 978-0-578-47489-2 (hardcover)

To my wife Ashley, who bought me my first camera when we were just kids in college and now is a loving mother to kids of our own. Thanks Ash for all your love and support.

Definiteness of purpose is the starting point of all achievement.

W. Clement Stone

Table of Contents

SOLD ON PURPOSE

MARKETING **TO THE CONSCIOUS** CONSUMER

The Feelings in a Box

It's finally here: a trip of a lifetime; an eventful kickstart to my freshman summer and, to my surprise, the birth of my professional career. While dropping off my bags at the airport, it finally set in that my long anticipated trip to the Dominican Republic had officially begun.

We are about to embark on a mission trip with the local church, but, selfishly, I see this as my first real adventure to a foreign land. A vacation to another world where I'll be cruising around an island for two weeks, and playing baseball with the locals. A time when I'll have the freedom to do whatever I want and not worry about homework or chores or any of the daily routines.

I'm daydreaming about all the exciting moments to come as the metronome of boarding passes being scanned in the distance gets closer and closer. Then, just as I'm about to board, one of the group leaders taps me on the shoulder and hands me a heavy gray box with a strap on the side of it. He explains, "Tim ... I need your help. For the people who don't go, the ones who won't see the conditions of these children or the scrap metal houses they live in. For all the people at home who will never experience what you experience on this trip, I need to capture all those moments and feelings and put them in this box, so when you get back, we can share it with them."

As he speaks, my attention is drawn fully to this mystery box. I'm flipping it in my hand, and as I slide one of the buttons, the box splits open. It looks like the top of a toaster. Then I see a familiar object inside. I realize that this antique is an old VHS camcorder. It's got buttons littered across the side of it, and as I experiment with the best way to hold this unwieldy contraption, I realize that you can't just slip the strap on one hand; you have to hug it with both hands because it constantly wants to fall to its side.

All my friends have taken their seats by now, but I'm still standing here, pretending to listen to this man. His words are being silenced by a bad feeling in my gut: the realization that this twenty-pound dumbbell is going to be strapped to my hand for the next two weeks.

"Sorry," I tell him. "I have no clue how to operate this thing. I've never even held a camera before, much less shot a movie in a foreign country."

He takes the camera back and, with his thumb back and his fingers to the sky, he slides the strap right down over his hand. He turns the camcorder on and explains, "It's easy. There's just one button here on the back, and when you click it, the light blinks red. Whatever you point at goes in, and whatever goes in comes home."

At this point, the flight attendant is giving the final call. The group leader hands me back the camera, and I sigh as I realize I have just become the "Video Guy" for the trip.

I turn and step toward the desk, but before I can take a second step, he taps me on the shoulder again. I turn around, already frustrated at his first request. With a smile, he raises a black bag and says, "You're going to need this." He's holding a gym bag full of VHS tapes and a *mountain* of batteries. My heart sinks. In the blink of an eye, this "vacation" has become a full-fledged work project. What was supposed to be a fun time with my friends will now be me babysitting the record button, acting as personal caddy to even more baggage.

As I go to my seat, the batteries clink and clank inside my bag with every step, drawing the attention of everyone on the plane to my late arrival.

Why in the world would anyone need so many batteries? I wonder as I take my seat. As we begin climbing into the clouds, I look out the window feeling like my trip has been hijacked.

We land in the capital, Santo Domingo, and the group splits up in buses to go to different cities. Some teams are going into the inner cities with baseball supplies for the kids. Some are going to the coastal towns with new clothes for families. My bus is to take the longest trek and travel to the rural border of the Dominican Republic and Haiti.

As I sit on the bus and toy with the camera, contemplating the burden thrust upon me, I discover something very peculiar as I look through the viewfinder. I had lived my entire life seeing the world through a wide-angle lens, but now, when I close one eye and look through the lens, it's like a telescope and the whole world becomes a little bit closer.

During the drive, I aim the camera at the passing trees and try to follow the motor scooters that speed by our bus. It turns into a game. For almost an hour, I try to hit targets with my eye, experimenting with every shot so I will be ready when the time comes to hit record. This is how I burned my first set of batteries—before we arrived.

Our first stop is a tin-roof village about a two-hour drive from Santo Domingo. As I walk in with our team, I raise the camera and press the little button on the back. Sure enough, the red light blinks, and I take my first shot. I zoom in on a scene of a mother hanging clothes on a line. I keep zooming closer and closer on her face until she looks at me and I can see into her eyes. It's as if we are nose to nose. And when she looks through the lens, it is as if she is looking right into my eyes, too. It is a closeness that is too intimate for any two strangers to exchange, so I turn the camera away. I move on to find my next shot, but I can't help but acknowledge that for a brief moment, I bridged the distance between myself and a stranger and found a unique sense of connection I have never quite experienced before.

The entire afternoon, I curiously capture the faces of people in the town. I record snippets of their lives. But in some of the best moments, I am interrupted by the camera shutting down, as it eats through several batteries a day. I end up wearing the battery bag like a belt of ammunition.

By the end of the day, I have fallen in love with seeing the world through the window of this camera. Over the next several days, I continue traveling around the island, getting a third-world education on capturing video as I examine the world through this new lens.

About halfway through the trip, I have almost used up my first VHS tape. We are approaching a new village, and I notice that the camera battery is at 5 percent, so I reach into the bag and suddenly realize I have made a critical error.

I'm out. I have used every battery, and there aren't any stores nearby where I can purchase more.

As we exit the bus and walk into the village, I execute the one trick I know. I begin to zoom in on the face of a little girl who is playing outside in the dirt. As she turns and looks into the lens, the expression in her eyes tells a story no words can convey. I continue zooming in closer and closer, trying to understand her expression, but the motors in the camera begin to slow down, and the picture fades to black.

Later, I realized I had made a major rookie mistake. I spent the rest of the trip without the camera. An entire bag of VHS tapes went unused, and I couldn't help but feel empty anytime I experienced a moment that I knew I couldn't bring back home. I wanted my little box back.

When we returned home, I volunteered to be the editor on the project—mainly so nobody would find out that I had only shot half the trip, but also because I was curious as to how this would all come together. I had learned iMovie in middle school, so I figured I could at least cut it together.

As I played the tape back from the VHS deck and recorded it to the church computer, I watched the moments play back like a puzzle on the screen. The scenes would come to life, then cut to shaky shots of a new location, then move to long segments where I forgot to hit the stop button, then back to shots of the remote village again.

A man named Ryan Kindle, who would become a longtime mentor, began to show me the art of placing the most meaningful moments side by side in the sequence and letting them dance to music. I learned that a great video isn't what you put in, but what shots you are willing to take out.

After three days of cutting and splicing and moving and tweaking, it was Saturday, and I just couldn't figure out how to make the video work. Making a video was more difficult than I ever expected, but I finally glued together two minutes of decent footage with an inspiring soundtrack that built up to the very end. As I put the final touches on it, a girl from the room next to me walked in and asked if she could watch it. I nodded and handed her the headphones as she moved close to the screen. I made the video full-screen and hit play. I had watched this video a thousand times during the edit, so this time, I just watched her.

The room was quiet. I could hear the soft echo of the song coming from her headphones. She stayed motionless throughout the entire video until the final scene. I watched her closely and saw her eyes begin to swell. As I looked closer, I could tell by the reflection in her eyes that it was the shot of the young Dominican child playing in the dirt. As the video slowly faded to black, I could see a tear rolling down her face, and I could tell by her reaction that she had stopped *watching* the video … and she had started *feeling* it. That was when I realized I wasn't making a video. I was making a feeling.

In that instant, the hairs on the back of my neck stood up as I finally understood what the man at the airport had asked me to do. I had become so distracted trying to get different angles and capture all the details that I had almost forgotten his simple request. My role wasn't to let people see what I saw, it was to let them feel what I felt. As he had so precisely explained it, I was there to capture feelings in the box.

As the video ended and I turned my attention to the black screen, she said, "We have to show this to the church."

The next day, during the Sunday evening service, the video played on the projection screen for everyone to see. The large screen and sound system amplified the experience that I had become so accustomed to viewing on a thirteen-inch monitor.

The images raced across the screen and the sound filled the room with emotion, but as the video came to an end, the room was dead silent. I felt a pit my stomach as the silence grew longer. The lights slowly came back up, and I could see some of the grown men and women in the congregation silently wiping away tears as if to hide their reactions. The applause followed shortly thereafter, and then as the pastor asked if anyone in the congregation would like to help, people left and right started pulling money out of their wallets to set in the offering plate.

I stood there, surprised by what I was seeing. These men and women were literally giving money to people they had never met, in a country they had never been to, for a cause they had never before seen. In the back of that church sanctuary, chills ran through my body again as I discovered what it felt like to inspire others.

They say the two most important days in your life are the day you're born and the day you find out why. That couldn't have been any truer for me. I would never in a million years have guessed that having an old VHS camera given to me in an airport terminal would change my entire life. Through that experience, it was clear to me that my purpose would be to inspire others through video.

That's the funny thing about **purpose**. Sometimes you find your purpose, and sometimes your purpose finds you.

While we're on the subject of purpose now, let me fill you in on what is to come. The purpose of this book is to **inspire a new era of marketers toward authentic, purpose-driven marketing**—a form of marketing meant to empower meaningful connections with brands and people and ultimately add value to humanity, rather than extract it.

Introduction

Right now, the year is 2019, and as I write this letter to my friends in the advertising world, it is very apparent that we are approaching a crisis of trust in America.

Many Americans have lost trust in the broadcast news and its dramatized interpretations of reality. They suspect infomercials and advertisements on TV to be exaggerations of the truth, and many are beginning to feel that even the daily highlight reels of their peers on social media are more like false positive moments rather than authentic depictions of real life. For these reasons and many others, authenticity in our digitally connected world is at an all-time low.

As famous storyteller Robert McKee suggests in his book *Storynomics*, we have created a world of **pseudo-stories.** Stories that have mutated in meaning and lack their true purpose. They are single-sided stories with either monotone upswings of positivity or downhill doses of negativity. Real, purposeful stories, on the other hand, are rollercoaster rides of highs and lows, that have moral lessons and meaningful insights. Great stories teach us about ourselves and the pattern of life. However, one look at modern storytelling in advertising today, and it's easy to see we've fallen off the tracks.

This book is intended to be a resource for getting purpose back into our stories. It is a roadmap for why your brand should champion purpose first and product second. And it provides a detailed way to structure your purpose story by using the same framework of the world's greatest stories.

Now, let's talk about what this book is not. This book is not a one-size-fits-all marketing solution. It's not meant to tell you your exact brand purpose or to be your only source of marketing knowledge. This book is more like a recipe for explaining your brand purpose and how this meaningful macro-story will play into all the multi-channel stories of your marketing.

Trying to time trends in a marketplace is like trying to measure the shoreline. The tides of attention and perception are always changing, more so today than ever before. Over time, fads change and trends die. This principle of brand purpose, however, is built on the existential longing that consumers have for understanding true meaning.

Purpose, then, at its core, is not marketing; it's meaning. While marketing seeks to answer **what**, purpose seeks to answer **why**. I hope this book helps you craft a more meaningful brand and, ultimately, **sell on purpose**.

Chapter 1:

The Purpose-Told Story

On August 25, 2017, the waters rose on the banks of the Gulf of Mexico near Houston, Texas, as a Category 4 hurricane barreled toward the city. What would happen next would be one of the most devastating natural disasters Texas had ever experienced.

Hurricane Harvey forced over 30,000 people from their homes and resulted in an estimated $125 billion in damage. Yet, in the wake of this horrific natural disaster, something beautiful emerged.

Over 500 miles away, in a small town in Georgia, production in the Anheuser-Busch® southeast bottling factory came to a screeching halt. On an average business day, the factory canned and shipped over 50,000 gallons of beer an hour, but on that day, its workers were shuffled into a conference room and informed of a peculiar change in production. Their iconic Budweiser® cans were to be pulled off the line immediately, and a new line of cans were to be loaded onto the production line.

The next day, riding on rescue canoes and atop inflatable mattresses, families in the neighborhoods of northeast Houston made their way to emergency shelters and Red Cross trailers. Amid the final whistling winds of Hurricane Harvey, rescue teams wrapped survivors in warm blankets and handed them each a can of water bearing an undeniably familiar logo. A Budweiser® water can.

The decision by Anheuser-Busch® to shut down beer production at their southeastern plant in favor of producing canned water for the victims of Hurricane Harvey told the world that their purpose was far greater than making refreshing, ice-cold beer or being the "King of Beers." This purpose-driven storyline proved that they were willing to put aside their commercial endeavors to help those in need when the hard times hit.

The next year, this story was shared in a heart-warming, sixty-second commercial that aired during the Super Bowl. The response was overwhelming. Social media began to buzz. People around the world felt connected to this cause on a level we had never before seen in a marketing effort. What Budweiser® had done was perceived as a heroic act of corporate responsibility, and it became an incredible brand message to millions.

What many viewers didn't realize was that Anheuser-Busch® had been donating water to disaster relief efforts for decades. Their Budweiser® Water Donation Program had been a key element of their brand story since the 1980s. To date, Anheuser-Busch® has donated over 80 million cans of drinking water around the world, including providing water to victims of Hurricane Irma in Puerto Rico and Florida the same year as Hurricane Harvey.

But why did Anheuser-Busch® take the risk to make this the central story of their Super Bowl commercial? Why did they decide that this would be their best marketing strategy for the most-watched game of the year? The beer giant could have easily produced a gimmicky ad to cement the Budweiser® brand in the minds of viewers or showed mouth-watering shots of their product to create desire. Instead of those tried-and-true tactics, they marketed their brand's purpose and delicately placed it in the heart of viewers—without ever showing a beer. Can you imagine trying to pitch that to the CEO? "We want to buy a $10 million extended Super Bowl ad … and not show our product."

While this all may sound crazy, it worked. This is a great case study for **cause marketing** because it evidences a key shift in modern advertising as we know it. The campaign increased the brand's perception dramatically for several months following the Super Bowl, particularly in the areas affected by hurricanes. Although brands have been marketing their values and purposes for years, the massive success of the Budweiser® Super Bowl commercial was proof of concept, on the largest platform, that you really can **"Sell On Purpose."**

Sold on Profit

Brand purpose is bigger than beliefs or values. Brand purpose is the calling. Ultimately, brand purpose is a brand's higher meaning for existence in the world. So why is it that so many brands don't know their own purpose? The quick answer is that they haven't needed to.

In the past, brands have been fortunate enough to operate in a unidirectional economy with a thick line between the brand and the consumer. Audiences had little to no voice, so they tolerated the purpose of profit as a universal driver for brands. Well, not anymore.

> **Brands have to stop thinking in terms of products and services and start thinking in terms of drivers and purposes.**

These days, consumers aren't just buying products from brands. They are buying the promise of what that brand will do for the world. This is an era of **conscious consumerism** where

25

the purchasing decision is now much more complex than ever before. Consumers are now buying based on the values they believe in. Author Anna Lappe said it this way: "Every time we spend money, we're casting a vote for the kind of world we want." The Budweiser® commercial was simply proof of timing.

Now, here we are, in a new, purpose-driven economy, on the brink of the biggest content explosion in the history of the modern world. The floodgates of purpose-driven marketing have let loose, horizontal marketing is the new norm, and the opportunity to have meaningful conversations with consumers is more open now than ever before. The question is, will brands shift away from the old pseudo-stories of the past and embrace purpose-driven storytelling to share their messages? Or will they continue to force-feed exaggerated direct advertising on consumers?

Because of social media, digitization, and the empowerment of the consumer's voice, we are entering a paradigm shift in marketing. The old rules of the past are quickly being rewritten. The new marketplace is begging for brands to stop interrupting what people are interested in and to *become* what people are interested in.

Today more than ever, CR is the new PR.

Corporate social responsibility is a concept that was originally built around the idea of sustainability. It arose during a time when consumers started asking questions like, "How ethical are companies when it comes to their waste?" Or, "How sustainable are these big corporations with their energy and water consumption?"

Corporate responsibility has since taken on a new social aspect. Today, CR—or what is now being commonly referred to as CSR—is something that consumers expect and demand from big business. When a natural disaster strikes, it's not a question of *if* the company responds, but *how* responsive they are.

What we're finding is that CR is attracting a lot of earned media attention. In the old days, **public relations** (PR) would focus on awards or maybe even charitable donations to evidence their impact on society. What we're now seeing, however, is that corporate responsibility is built around **tangible actions**. It's not about monetary gifts. It's about what a company actually *does* when the world needs them.

This is a core concept of the purpose-told story because it's putting values into action. There's no better way to be authentic than to do what you say. And so, at a time when brands are more exposed than ever before, it's very important that companies not only market their values, but act on them.

In the traditional marketing model, brands controlled the marketplace with **vertical advertising**. They could force-feed advertisements to consumers by interrupting their desired content. But in the new, digitally connected world, **audience fragmentation** and digitization have created a more informed and elusive consumer base. **Over-the-top media services (OTT)** now allow consumers an ad-free experience with subscriptions such as Netflix® and Amazon Prime Video®. Over 300 million ad blockers have been installed on computers worldwide to prevent digital advertising online.

What used to be a vertically controlled marketplace for advertising has been turned on its side. Now, in the **horizontal marketplace**, consumers are marketing to other consumers about their experiences through product reviews and social media posts. As forecasted by marketing legend Philip Kotler in his book *Marketing 3.0*, we have entered the **Participation Age**, where a hyperconnected world of consumers can now actively participate in a more global marketplace. Social media has connected the peer-to-peer channels across the globe, allowing consumers to market on the same scale as brands.

> **For the first time in history, consumers are taking control of the marketplace, and public perception is now the currency that drives this market.**

In the new digital marketplace, consumers desire brand connections not based on exaggerations of products or services, but on a deeper level through values and purpose. Today, consumers value purpose over price and consider *process* to be just as important as *product*. This eco-friendly, gender-neutral, energy-efficient, chemically-conscious society is migrating toward higher social mentalities in the marketplace and using **collective opinion** as purchasing power. Consumers yelling through their digital megaphones of social media and consumer reviews represent the new age of brand campaigns.

Since consumers are telling consumers the real story of the brand, brands no longer own the message of *what* they do. The only message brands control is *why* they do it. The message of purpose is one that only the brand can tell.

1.1 The Story of Stories

Since the beginning of time, stories have been used as humanity's toolkit for understanding. Oral storytelling around campfires gave ancient humans the unique ability to understand life without having to experience it first—something no other animal can do. This evolutionary advancement allowed each new generation to build on what the previous ones had achieved, advancing society at an incredible rate.

Then, 2,500 years ago, a technological breakthrough made it easier than ever to share stories. Traders in Ancient Persia trekked across the desert carrying sheepskin manuscripts bearing the primal beginnings of written language. This was a game-changer. What began as a rudimentary system of record-keeping soon led to the dissemination of stories from one village to another. From this moment on, the idea of shared storytelling transcended location and exploded across all cultures in the world. The written word gave storytellers the ability to spread their tales across continents and over oceans, and the greatest stories ever told became accessible on a global scale.

With the invention of the printing press in the 1800s, we had access to more ideas and stories, which compounded ideation at an exponential rate, spawning the development of the Industrial Age. During this time, our attention was fixated on newspapers and books. This new, sprawling medium of content was flourishing. Oral storytelling was a thing of the past. Parents scolded their kids for spending too much time with their heads in books and encouraged them to get out and play "like in the good old days."

But we didn't stop. We were hooked on good stories, and now that a new newspaper could be printed every other week, there were always fresh and relevant stories ready for us to consume.

This story had only just begun.

From the Print to the Pictures

As the newspaper continued to gain popularity, advancements paved the way for a new storytelling medium called radio. By tuning and translating distant radio waves into an audible frequency, the radio receiver instantaneously captured the voices of people speaking hundreds of miles away and transmitted them right into our homes.

With radio, we could hear stories like never before. Why travel to a theater in the city to see a play when you could listen to one from the comfort of your own home? Now, we didn't need to wait two weeks to get the news in written form. This magic box could play stories all night long. The pendulum of storytelling swung again—from oral to written back to oral—and audio was king.

Radio became so popular that in the early 1900s, programming was broadcast all day and night. After a few more years, multiple networks were born, and stories began to compete for airtime against music-only programming. Families gathered around their radio to get the day's news and to listen to their favorite entertainment programs. In 1938, Orson Welles directed and narrated a radio broadcast version of "The War of the Worlds," and widespread pandemonium broke out when listeners, who failed to hear the disclaimer that it was a fictional story, believed they were listening to a news broadcast of the world coming to an end. While this was a rather frightening event for many listeners, it provided a very interesting revelation for marketers in the 20th century.

During this time, another storytelling format was becoming popular. Moving pictures became the new focus for great stories. In the early 1900s, black-and-white images raced across the screen, and audiences were, amazingly, able to translate the sequences of moving light as living scenes. These modern-day hieroglyphics in motion became the highest-quality form of storytelling to date.

The Big Screens Get Smaller

The big screen was bringing stories to life as real as we had ever seen. The film stock progressed to color, and audio was played in sync with the visuals to create a multisensory experience. This exciting form of entertainment advanced our species once again. We had transcended oral communication to the written word, to audio, and now to video, but by the late

40s, a new medium was emerging that would revolutionize modern storytelling as we knew it.

Televisions hit the consumer market in the 1950s, and after several years of bunny ears and fuzzy images, the TV evolved into a realistic colorized representation of life. Broadcast waves filled the air as this small metal box with a window on the front became a common appliance in almost every household. Parents once again scolded their kids for being glued to a new-fangled device—the tube—but kids and adults alike couldn't look away. Year after year, it changed shapes and sizes. New advancements transformed it from a heavy, vacuumed tube of projected light into a flat, wall-mounted display no thicker than the average book.

Over time, this ever-evolving window to the world began to shape our thoughts and perceptions. It was influencing our culture and, more importantly, our beliefs. What started out as a single-station TV now had thousands of channels and networks for anything and everything. This created a widespread entertainment addiction. TVs were put in every room in the house. They littered the insides of schools, offices, and hospitals. Hospitals even put TVs in the birthing rooms for the expectant parents.

The Birth of Boob-Tube Advertising

Many kids growing up in the following decades would be exposed to television in some way every day of their lives. Our species, which had evolved so rapidly over the last 200 years, became slaves to the screen.

Businesses capitalized on this mind-numbing medium by inserting propaganda about their products into the storylines. Cartoon character Fred Flintstone smoked Winston® cigarettes. Olympic athletes drank brightly branded sports drinks on the sidelines. Soon, it was commonplace and even accepted that during the most suspenseful, climactic parts of a show, advertisers interrupted the feed and switched to artificially sweetened stories of how fantastic life would be if you bought their products.

Commercials became commonplace on TV, but they were only pseudo-stories, so consumers couldn't connect with them as much as they did with the stories that were interrupted. These half-baked stories began to mutate over time as advertisers saw the opportunity to use them for conditioning the gullible masses. Advertisers funded research in emotional manipulation techniques to increase the efficiency of their persuasion. Politicians began buying the attention pool just before elections to saturate breaks during family-friendly programming with ad hominem attack ads that undermined the integrity of their opponents—then paid multi-network news stations to talk about it the following week.

A strange thing began to happen. Networks realized that shows gained viewership the more provocative they became. The generation who had seen and heard it all began to crave conflict and controversy. So, like any good drug dealer, the networks gave it to them. News networks fueled their storylines with negativity and exaggerations of events. One reporter famously remarked, "In news, if it bleeds, it leads!" This kamikaze mind machine was now on autopilot, and our collective, undivided attention fueled its fateful descent. What was initially a promising advancement in communication had degenerated into a one-way information stream through which TV shaped our view of the world.

The Genie in the Bottle

Henry Ford is said to have famously remarked, "If I would have asked people what they wanted, they would have said a faster horse." Surely, if the TV generation had been asked what they wanted, they would have said, "a bigger big-screen." Instead, the screens mounted on the walls in our houses migrated to the pockets of our pants. The TV screen, which had been growing bigger and bigger each year, shrank to a five-inch portable screen on our phones. No need for hardwired power or cables. This convenient new screen could be used by toddlers and adults alike.

Society embraced these devices as the natural progression of the phone. After a short time, cordless screens had our attention tied up and strangled. Just like the generations of the past, our intuition told us that we should prevent our kids from staring at these mini-TVs all day, so parents initially scolded youths for having their noses in the screens all day. But what was the harm, really? After all, we all grew up glued to the TV set, and this new, digital-native generation was so well-behaved when watching these little handheld storytellers.

Many of the commercials *on* these miniature screens were *about* these miniature screens. New screens. Higher-definition screens. Faster, better, stronger screens. Ads played daily that showed hero stories of how video-streaming phones helped connect faraway families and taught kids through video with some of the most entertaining teachers who ever lived. It seemed there was nothing that these pocket tablets couldn't do, and we were all so happy with them. By all appearances, disconnecting in person didn't matter; we were all more connected through our screens.

But over time, we isolated our experiences with these devices. We wore headphones in public and walked with our heads down. New media offered the promise that wherever we were, we could be somewhere better with a push of a button. Instead of the old days of waiting for stories that played at times chosen by the broadcaster, we could play whatever we wanted whenever we wanted.

No bigger than a TV remote itself, our new controllers gave us the power we were longing for: the world's vast collection of stories all filed neatly into a small, white search bar. No Dewey Decimal System needed in this library—you could literally just type in what you wanted, and in seconds, it would appear. After a few years, you didn't even need to type anymore. Like a genie in a magic bottle, your phone would wake up at your command, and you could ask it to give you anything you wanted, from toilet paper to a diamond ring. Just ask, and it would be delivered in two days!

At last! This was the thing we had always wanted.... Right?

Something suddenly felt wrong. All the images and sounds and storylines were there, but something was missing. A piece of the puzzle had vanished, leaving the experience feeling inauthentic.

Simply put, it had lost its **purpose**.

1.2 The Millennial Movement

What a story! From petroglyphs on cave walls to emotionally charged videos on screens that fit in your pockets, our medium for storytelling continued to evolve. But—spoiler alert! Our desire for control and connectedness ended up leaving us feeling more powerless and disconnected than ever before.

The evidence is all around us. We have begun to realize that the instant attainment of our every desire leaves the sense of the journey unfulfilled. Being digitally connected to friends and family twenty-four hours a day is no substitute for real-life time together.

The TV, which crept its way into the fabric of our lives seventy years ago and brought families together, has evolved into something that leaves us feeling isolated and empty. Today, much to the chagrin of their parents, the younger generation is taking it upon themselves to rectify this.

While we have adapted the stories we tell today for a new-age audience, we are approaching an era in which the changes in storytelling techniques are critical for more effective connections—and effective advertising. The techniques of the past are losing their effectiveness, and brands are left with two options: sink or learn to swim.

The New Norm: Media on Demand

Today, more media is being uploaded and consumed than ever before. Over 8 billion hours of video content is uploaded across the internet every day. YouTube® reported in 2018 that, on average, over 5 billion YouTube® videos are watched each day. This is insane. There is so much media in the marketplace, yet the supply *still* cannot keep up with the demand. It is truly a great time to be a marketer or an advertiser.

The problem is, the landscape has completely changed. Everything that advertising experts learned over the past fifty years about traditional mass media marketing is rapidly evolving. We are transcending the broadcast age.

In the broadcast age, you could buy a TV ad and be assured that you were placing your messages in peoples' heads. You *knew* that TV had the attention of your audience every night. A family gathered around their favorite show, captivated by a great story, was certain to see your thirty-second brand message and "stay tuned" to see how the show ended.

Even back in the 1950s, at the dawn of the broadcast age, this was not a new concept. When Benjamin Franklin invented **interruptive advertising** in the late 1700s, it was a very practical idea. Instead of advertising on the front page or the side column of the newspaper, Franklin observed that an advertisement placed right in the middle of an article gained the most attention because the viewer was already actively engaged in the story. This model worked so well that it continued to be used in radio and was introduced to broadcast TV.

In the early years of TV, this worked quite well. Audiences had no problem watching commercials as a courtesy to the network, since the programming was free. But now, we are being asked to pay for cable and satellite packages, and we're still stuck enduring the ads too! Not to mention that the frequency and duration of TV ads have increased by 200 percent in the last twenty-five years.

This eighteenth-century model is outdated. It just doesn't make sense in the new digital world we live in. Let's be honest. Do you want someone nagging you about your medical insurance in the middle of listening to your favorite song on the radio? Or someone trying to sell you a car during the most exciting moment of your TV show? Nobody wants that—not even the marketers who create the ads! In the old days, we were stuck with it. We couldn't escape advertising because it was the price we had to pay to watch our favorite shows or listen to our favorite music or even drive the most convenient route to work.

But now, we are in the middle of a major transition. Many households have cut out cable completely, and the Millennial generation is dropping it faster than anyone else, opting for on-demand OTT platforms like Netflix®, Hulu®, Amazon Prime Video®, HBO Go®, etc. The landscape has changed.

The Fyre of Social Marketing

As the traditional channels of media are becoming inferior to their new alternative equivalents, social media has become an arena where consumers can connect to other consumers and get a more grounded perspective of reality. However, in 2017, Fyre Festival spoiled this medium as well.

In December of 2016, Fyre Festival was announced as the biggest new music festival to hit the scene. Co-founders Billy McFarland and rapper Ja Rule began promoting it as the premier music festival of our century for Millennials, complete with luxury accommodations and exotic cuisine. As they began to take the idea to market, they flew down to the Bahamas with a group of America's top models and posted behind-the-scenes videos of the island where the festival would take place. They paid the models to post on their social media channels to influence their platforms and legitimize the festival's existence.

Once they had their promotional material in place, they hired several other social media influencers to post that they were beyond excited to attend the upcoming Fyre Festival. They reportedly even paid Kendall Jenner $250,000 to post on Instagram® that artists from Kanye West's record label, G.O.O.D Music®, would be performing and she couldn't wait to go. Just two days after the social media blitz, the festival was almost sold out. After all, on social media it sounded like the experience of a lifetime. And everyone was going, right?

Wrong.

Five months later, when the festival finally kicked off, the grim reality set in. Guests were appalled to discover that none of the celebrity guests were in appearance. The festival's luxury accommodations consisted of old FEMA tents, and the exotic cuisine turned out to be cheese sandwiches. In fact, the entire experience was so unbearable that it was canceled altogether by the second day, and everyone was sent back home.

How could all this happen? All the influencers we trusted on social media said they were going! And videos and pictures online made it seem like an incredible event. But in the end, it was just smoke and mirrors. A $100 million lawsuit quickly ensued, and today, Billy McFarland is spending six years behind bars for fraud. The Fyre Festival showed the world that even social media can be influenced by the same fairy-tale advertising that has plagued the TV screen for years. The same larger-than-life lies that were being sold to us in between our favorite shows were now hidden in our social feeds, disguised as posts by people we trusted. We quickly came to understand these social media influencers were the modern day form of the info-mercial TV hosts of the past. New platform, but same old tricks.

Today, consumers are the advertisers of the future, increasing the complexity of trust and understanding in the marketplace.

The Backlash against Traditional Marketing

After years of being deceived by empty promises from advertisers, consumers have come to understand that traditional advertising is no more than propaganda for advancing products to market.

For example, a popular technique in broadcast marketing is the use of **neuro-linguistic programming (NLP)**. NLP is the way that words are heard and interpreted in the subconscious. The concept is based on the notion that certain words can influence or even command one's subconscious. For instance, a well-known battery commercial says, "By now—nine out of ten doctors trust XXXX as the best brand." If you take that apart and dissect it, you'll realize that the first two words are a **subliminal command clause.** "By now," or what's being heard as "*buy* now," is orienting the mind in the purchasing decision before the brand is even introduced.

The phrase "nine out of ten doctors" is also a well-established NLP strategy called **social confirmation** or **peer validation**. When you hear this, be assured that it isn't some random study that was created. This is a hack on a universal behavioral phenomenon. We know that humans do as they see, and furthermore, they behave the way they see groups behave. If you were to walk outside and one person was looking up in the sky, you might think they were crazy, but if nine out of ten people were looking up, you wouldn't even question the group. You would look up as well. It's a subtle but powerful technique that advertisers use to make things seem more truthful.

Another technique used here is good-ole' expert advice. When the ad says that "doctors trust" the battery brand, the mind associates the authority and intelligence of a doctor's decision as being more informed than their own. So, without any external research, the mind can assume, "If most doctors trust it, so can I." As you can see here though, this ad is just a novel play on words to influence the mind. Using NLP and other clever wording techniques is an age-old strategy to say what the viewer wants to hear without making any claims that would put the brand in jeopardy.

During the broadcast era, another advertising technique that worked especially well was **inadequacy marketing**. Advertisements would metaphorically tell the consumer, "You're not good enough," by showing a life the consumer wished they could have and creating envy for that lifestyle. Through repetition, consumers would begin to associate the product as the key to acquiring that lifestyle. Once the pain grew large enough, they would be primed for purchase.

Aristotle famously said, "The aim of the wise is not to secure **pleasure**, but to avoid **pain**." The inadequacy marketing approach is exactly that. It is death by a thousand paper cuts, planting envy in the mind of consumers and watering it daily with multi-channeled reminders. You've probably seen it a million times before—maybe you've even created ads like this yourself. The following are three real commercials that are broken down into the "inadequacy message" that the brand is sending, followed by the call-to-action.

Inadequacy Marketing

- *An athlete trains fiercely in the gym, day after day, trying to beat his personal record. He punches his locker as he is calloused with defeat. With his head down, he sees a new box at the bottom of his rusty locker that he's never seen before, and he slowly opens it to reveal a new pair of sneakers and blasts off faster than ever to achieve his record time.*
  - "You're not fast enough. Buy these shoes."
- *A young, wealthy man in a convertible sports car with a beautiful lady in the front seat slowly drives by as everyone on the street corner turns their heads. He winks at a boy standing alone on the opposite corner as if to say, "You could have this life, too." The boy appears enlightened as he realizes that someday, maybe he can buy an expensive car to earn the admiration of his peers and marry a beautiful woman as well.*
  - "You're not cool enough. Buy this car."
- *A girl walks the hallways of her school, being laughed at by her peers, then runs into the bathroom where she rips open her bag and begins putting on a new, bold shade of lipstick. She walks the hallway again and, in slow motion, the jaws of her peers drop open. They stand motionless, and the girl smiles as the boy of her dreams walks toward her with wonder.*
  - "You're not pretty enough. Buy this makeup."

While we've all seen these stereotypical types of ads and may even laugh at their exaggerated attempts to persuade consumers, don't discount the negative effects inadequacy marketing has had on our society. Since 1970, eating disorders among young women have increased by over 400 percent and credit card debt continues to increase year after year because of ads motivating irresponsible consumerism. The most vulnerable population for these types of advertisements are adolescents who, during development, can be permanently influenced by these pseudo-stories. Countless studies have shown that children who watch violent shows are much more aggressive and prone to violence in school settings than children who don't. This is because, as humans, we are built to imitate what we see. Showing stories of the main character being inadequate without a certain product can elicit the same thought process and behavior.

The main recurring theme found in inadequacy marketing is that the brand is always the hero. In the examples above, the car brand makes a boring life exciting, the shoe brand makes a slow runner fast, and the makeup brand makes an undesirable girl desirable. The assumed context then, is that without the car, your life will be boring, without the shoe, you'll never be fast, and without the makeup, you'll never be desirable. These are the subconscious stories used by these types of ads to prey on the insecurities of consumers. Fortunately, recent studies indicate that the Millennial generation is actually having an adverse response to these types of ads.

Because the Millennial generation is so hyperconnected to information, inadequacy marketing techniques are proving to be ineffective. In some cases, inadequacy marketing negatively impacts Millennials' perception of a brand.

Simon Sinek said it best in his 2009 book, *Start With Why*: "There are only two ways to influence human behavior: You can either manipulate it, or you can inspire it." We are starting to turn the corner from manipulative messaging toward inspirational messaging. We're moving from the inadequacy marketing model to the **empowerment marketing** model.

The main idea of empowerment marketing is that you position the consumer or the cause as the hero in the story, not the brand. You tell people that they already have all the potential they need and that they can change the world. The brand is simply the cheerleader or mentor to help in their journey. Here are the same examples, now communicated using the empowerment model.

Empowerment Marketing

- *"These shoes will help the whole world run better."*
  Since 2015, Adidas® has teamed up with Parley Ocean Plastic Program to create the "Run for the Ocean" movement, which funds ocean cleanup efforts and uses the recovered plastics to create shoes. The week-long event brings awareness to harmful waste in the ocean. Adidas® also launches its new line of recovered plastics shoes during that week and the profits from these shoes go directly to the cleanup program, making it a sustainable shoe. Instead of trying to make the costumer run faster, they are empowering the consumer to be a part of a higher purpose, and participate in ridding the world of harmful plastic waste, in turn, making the whole world 'run' better.

- *"You are amazing, and we want to drive with you."*
  In 2017, Ford® created the ad campaign "Welcome to the driver's seat" in response to Saudi Arabia lifting its ban on women drivers. The ad prominently featured a Muslim woman's eyes looking in the rear-view mirror directly at the audience. This simple ad said nothing about Ford® or their vehicles, but everything about what they believed. It sent a message of hope to a population group that has been oppressed for hundreds of years. They sent the message that

they believe women should be given equal rights in everything in life.

- *"You are beautiful, and we want to help you feel as beautiful as you are."*

  In 2004, Dove® launched the "Real Beauty" campaign that swept the nation. Their ads featured real life women of all shapes, colors, and sizes, and proved to the world that women are beautiful just the way they are. By showing what makes us unique also makes us beautiful, Dove® was making a bold call-to-belief about beauty. For over 15 years now, this has become an empowering message to the masses.

These types of stories are often affirmations of the human spirit and leave the audience feeling inspired afterward. In 2013, Dove® created an extension of their already brilliant "Real Beauty" campaign called "Inner Beauty." They designed a social experiment where women would describe how they looked to a forensic artist. The artist could not see their faces, but instead, created drawings based on personal descriptions from the women. As an added twist to the experiment, Dove® revealed that another person would meet these women in the lobby before they went in to talk to the artist. Those people were then asked to give a description to the artist of how *they* perceived the women. The final result was two images side by side. One of how the women saw themselves, and another of how the world perceived them.

The conclusion of the experiment was that most women were very hard on themselves and didn't describe the beauty that the other people saw in them. Dove® showed the audience that these women were blind to their own inner beauty. It made a powerful statement: The world finds you beautiful, even if you don't see it yourself. This message was one that resonated so much with female audiences that it went viral in just a couple days after release. In fact, the message was so compelling that Dove® gained tens of millions of views online without having to pay the price of having to advertise it because their audience was sharing it for them. This is what great stories do, they connect to consumers on an emotional level, and teach them a greater truth about the world and themselves. Ultimately, we are moving in a direction in advertising that rewards truly empowering content like this and it is a great lesson that all brands can learn.

1.3 The Challenge: Sharing Your Message in the Post-Broadcast World

Now, with the onset of digitization, consumers are free from most of the chains of traditional mass media. We are free from the interruptive yell-and-sell tactics of the past. From the all-in-one onion slicer info-mercials to the exotic fruit creams that promised to give you wrinkle-free skin and the stain-fighting detergents that make old, dingy clothes brand new again. These commercialized, larger-than-life product claims have been exposed by consumer reviews, turning one-hit-wonders into overnight lawsuits.

The broadcast marketing tactics of the past, including product puffery, no longer resonate with the new generations of consumers because they can fact check on the spot. False claims by a brand can not only be proven false by consumers, but also can turn into an overnight PR nightmare. The research is now clear that Millennial and Gen Z audiences don't want to be interrupted while consuming content. The entire idea of interrupting an audience's experience to play a forced ad is becoming a thing of the past. In fact, recent studies are indicating that prolonged interruptive advertising can have a negative brand impression on your audience.

> Audiences are begging brands to stop interrupting what they are interested in and instead become what they are interested in.

Fortunately, the advertising industry is hearing their cries and making a dramatic shift away from exaggerating their products and forcing interruptive ads on their audiences. Innovative brands are now offering useful and entertaining content that is available on the audience's terms. While the content may appear ad-free to the audience, it is a form of disguised, **branded entertainment**, which has a major impact on the viewer's perception of the brand.

This **content marketing** mindset is one that energy drink giant Red Bull® does better than anyone else (which we'll discuss in more detail in Chapter 9).

The Purpose-Told Story

Marketers who value quantity of views over quality connections are trading short-term gains for a long-term loss. Impressions will always be inferior to expressions. The spray-and-pray age of amplifying crappy content to your audience may drive the view count up on your analytics, but real, purposeful stories, well told, will reciprocate themselves through the proverbial grapevine.

> In the digital world, people don't need to depend on the advice of brands to tell them what to do. They can conduct powerful independent research in moments from their smartphones. As a result, Millennials value individuality, creativity, and authenticity.

The Purpose-Told Story is all about providing the deeper meaning to an audience. It is the story of Why. There are over 80 million Millennial Americans, and more than any other generation, Millennials long for purpose. They don't buy *what* you do. They buy *why* you do it.

Millennials are looking for a sense of identity and purpose in the brands they follow. While many marketers are continuing to market based on commands and calls to actions, purpose-driven brands illustrate their identity to what they believe in. They use methods like **cause marketing** to communicate their beliefs through action and let the consumer see the higher meaning of their brand. Just like Budweiser's® canned water commercial and Dove's® Inner Beauty campaign, brands that live their purpose are rewarded greatly by consumers.

> **Brands that Sell on Purpose don't make a call to action. Instead, they create a call to belief.**

If the viewer believes in your cause, you don't have to tell them what to do. They will figure it out by themselves. By not being guided by your commands, this inherently gives them the very independence they are seeking.

The Orientation Effect

While content marketing, branded entertainment, and cause marketing are all great ways to connect to your audience in the new age of advertising, there is one key factor that is needed to make all these strategies effective—one factor that makes the connection even possible—and that is purpose. When you align your purpose with your message and your audience, you are activating something called the **orientation effect**.

In chemistry, the **orientation effect** occurs when elements with the right orientation bond and create a compound. In marketing, this same effect occurs when a brand's purpose and a viewer's values bond. They link up to create a compound that is oriented toward the brand message.

> **By connecting *first* to the audience on shared values and *then* presenting the message, it gives greater leverage to the message.**

This strategy simply orients the viewer to be more accepting of the message. The reason for this is that the more consumers believe in the purpose of a brand, the less objectively critical they will be about the messages it sends. Connect with existing values first, then introduce greater value interpretations.

Sounds obvious, right? It is pretty darn close to one of the most basic principles of marketing your message: Align your company's core offerings with your target audience's needs and tell them about it over and over.

However, purpose-driven content in the connected world is no easy task. The small nuances of micro-positioning and order of delivery make a major difference. In the next chapter, we examine the details of purpose, the psychology behind decision-making, and human beings' biological need for a sense of purpose.

Chapter 2:

Our Biological Need for Purpose – How Humanity's Innate Desire for Meaning Drives Decision-Making

Thousands of years ago, humans relied heavily on their observatory senses for survival. Whether it was seeing danger hidden in a dark cave, noticing a change in weather conditions, or hearing the quiet rustling of an approaching predator, we have relied on our senses over time to help protect us and better understand the world around us.

As we evolved, our senses allowed us to create dynamic insights about reality. It was no longer purely about survival. There was joy and beauty to be experienced by seeing, hearing, smelling and tasting. There is one sense however, that has always and will always dominate them all. It is the sense of feeling—not the sense of tactile touch that gives us the ability to observe texture or temperature, but the internal feeling of emotion. How we feel is the state of being that guides our minds in decision-making. How we feel is often, in large part, the result of a prediction based on past experiences. For example, standing on a cliff you may feel scared, not because you are falling, but because you predict that you could fall. So, you feel that way because you predict you should feel that way.

> **Past experience is the canvas on which we paint new observations.**

Without past experiences, we have no reference for understanding. But, as I mentioned in Chapter 1, the power of storytelling is that it enables humans to understand life without experiencing it first. If a young hunter has grown up hearing stories told by his father and grandfather, tales recounting the behavior of prey and predators in the wild, he can one day venture forth armed with the knowledge of prior generations. This second-hand experience becomes his equipment for survival. Let's dig a little into the science of how we perceive purpose.

2.1 The Biology of Meaning

Scientists will tell you that our eyes don't see images and our ears don't hear sounds. Rather, it's the mind that's the active observer, using the unconscious tool of the eye to translate light waves into recognizable visual patterns and the ear to collect incoming audio frequencies and interpret them by comparing them to past familiar sounds.

In this process, the brain is simply the record of past experiences, the hard drive of old data. The mind is the conscious conductor moving throughout the brain and tapping into our observatory tools to create connections between past and present. Therefore, the mind provides understanding based on observation—the ultimate sensor of meaning. The mind is always looking for meaning.

For example, let's say you are on a nature walk and in a split second, your eyes see a four-legged animal with fur. Your mind begins to sift through the records of the brain for past experiences to identify the meaning and predict the purpose of the event.

Based on the observation and the record of experiences, you can determine whether the four-legged, furry creature is a friendly poodle who wants to say hello or a ravenous wolf looking for his next meal. Then, based on that deduction, the mind can supply the appropriate emotion to the body. While this sounds like a simple idea, it's important to know that consumers are using the same split-second processes of deciphering meaning when they see your product. They may not truly know your brand, so they are leaning on generic associations to understand your purpose.

In a famous research study in the early 2000s, researchers divided a pile of blue pills and orange pills onto a table. The test subjects were given one of the two pills and were to be monitored overnight for a sleep experiment. The researchers recorded the activity of the subjects and came to a very peculiar discovery. Although both the blue pills and the orange pills were placebos, the subjects who were given the blue placebo pill went to sleep faster and stayed asleep longer than subjects who were given the orange placebo pill. You may be wondering, if both pills were placebos, how can this be?

The answer is that the subjects believed the purpose of the blue pill was to help them sleep, so it affected their behavior and made them feel more tired. That is the power of how the mind applies meaning. This is an important illustration because it shows how the mere perception of an object's purpose can physically affect the way we feel about it.

Cavemen and Confetti

Initially, purpose was a mechanism used purely for survival. Perceiving meaning helped the minds of ancient human beings predict whether an object or situation would be helpful or harmful to their existence.

In the early 70s, researchers studied the effect that confetti had on different cultures around the world. When a single piece of confetti (a confetto) was shown, subjects demonstrated little to no emotional reaction. A small, colored piece of paper meant nothing to them. However, when they were shown a cloud of colorful confetti, almost all of the subjects lit up with emotion and increased brain activity in the areas of the brain associated with fulfillment and satisfaction.

The interesting thing about this is that many of the cultures examined had no **learned association** with confetti, unlike the previous blue pill example. These participants, who had never seen confetti thrown into the air at a birthday party or shot from cannons on New Year's Eve, were feeling the same way as those who had developed that learned association. Why?

After years of looking for answers, the researchers concluded that the colorful abundance of flying paper traces back to our prehistoric roots. Thousands of years ago, when early humans migrated from cave to cave, their observations of the land would guide their decision-making regarding where to settle. When a tribe saw an area of colorful, fruitful abundance, it would trigger an innate understanding that an area was good for them; on the other hand, a desolate wasteland devoid of color would evoke a sense of despair.

Researchers made the link that the colorful confetti, much like a colorful, flourishing field of fruits and berries, triggered a divine sense of well-being. This was the mind's way of giving purpose to observation. The subjects weren't just perceiving flying, colorful paper. It wasn't just a stimulus of surprise. They were sensing abundance, and the universal purpose of that sense of abundance was good for their overall well-being.

It's hard not to notice that today's advertisements are more colorful and louder than ever before. From the brightly colored sale signs that litter the aisles at grocery stores to the pulsing row of TVs lined up in the windows of electronic stores, the perception of abundance has been packaged through advertising and sold to us in bulk as a society over the years. So next time you see some colorful, flashing animation of deals dancing across your TV set between shots of shiny new cars, ask yourself, is this really showing who they are, or are they just throwing confetti?

"Gut Instinct" Chemistry

While the mind is the ultimate meaning-maker, it has the ability to move awareness throughout the body to collect information for understanding. One key area of the body that we all reference for decision-making is the gastrointestinal tract or the gut. Our gut is highly sensitive to emotion and is often a key factor in determining how we feel about an object or event.

Think about this in your own life. If you're anxious about speaking in front of a large group of people, you may get the sensation of "butterflies" in your stomach, or if you have a bad conscience because you did something wrong, you may feel literally "sick to your stomach." Often times, when someone has a resounding sense of confidence about something but doesn't have the logic to back it up, they'll say they have "a gut feeling."

Another interesting feeling in the gut is a physical sensation of weightlessness. In several languages and cultures around the world, people describe falling in love as being "swept off their feet" or "head over heels in love." This feeling of weight-lessness inspired by a sense of attraction toward another person is a real thing, and it all happens in the gut.

Here is an example of the simplified command chain in the body of a pleasurable experience. The mind commands the brain to order the hormone glands to secrete dopamine to the central nervous system, which delivers this chemical throughout the body to the vital organs and your gastro-intestines, which files this sense of pleasure in the unconscious memory bank of the body and correlates it with past meaning. It then sends the final signal of the reaction back to the mind. This record takes the form of intuition, or "a gut feeling," for future decisions. If you had a great experience with cake, your body will intuitively feel good when seeing it, and if you vomited while eating broccoli, your gut will send a clear signal that something isn't right the next time you see broccoli.

While your body remembers the emotion, it cannot remember all the data of the event like your brain does, so your gut reaction is often just an emotionally charged intuition based on the past. This will become important later on as we discuss the intuitive feelings your purpose story can evoke.

2.2 Classical Conditioning: Pavlov, Little Albert, and Fred Flintstone

At some point or another, you've probably come across the study of "Pavlov's dog." This is a reference to the theories of **classical conditioning** put forth by Russian scientist Ivan Pavlov in the 1890s. It had long been observed that when food was brought to dogs, they would salivate. The stimulus of the imminent meal had an effect on their biological processes, producing an **unconditioned response** to the stimulus of the food:

salivation. Pavlov introduced a bell that he rang each time he fed a dog. After a while, the dog salivated anytime it heard the bell ring, regardless of whether any food was present.

By ringing a bell every time he fed the dog, Pavlov had created **an association.** Over time, through repetition, he conditioned the association to produce the same response as the unconditioned stimuli.

- Unconditioned stimuli: the food
- Unconditioned response: salivation
- Associated stimuli: the bell

As you can imagine, classical conditioning has been used in advertising for decades. If you associate a product with something that gives you an unconditioned response, like a feeling, you can essentially derive a feeling from something that's not actually there. An example would be a McDonald's® billboard showing a very attractive lady holding a hamburger and smiling. Imagine the twenty-four-year-old male who drives past that billboard every day and is very attracted to this woman. He might not even be hungry for a hamburger (unconditioned stimuli), but the feelings outside of the context of what the ad is saying (the associated stimuli) are producing an unconditional response. When he's deciding where to eat, there's a little voice in the back of his mind that is associating the feeling he had of seeing that lady with the food.

Over time, associations created by advertising become strong enough that they condition our choices when we're making a purchase. A young woman in a convenience store who has been repeatedly shown Coke® commercials with smiling faces, is likely to choose a Coke® product over a competitors product. She's not consciously thinking, "Oh, this Coke's® going to make me happy," but in the back of her mind, that's a real part of the decision-making process, and it's constantly happening behind the scenes. People will use what they have seen through repetition with unconditioned responses over and over, rather than those that they're unfamiliar with.

The Dark Side of Conditioning

Something that evolved out of Pavlov's research was the "Little Albert experiment" in the 1920s, in which psychologist John B. Watson set out to create a conditioned phobia in an infant.

We know that infants and young children are scared of loud noises. Their natural response is to cry or to try to run away. For Watson's experiment, he would sit a nine-month-old boy named Little Albert down and allow him to play with a harmless, white lab rat. Watson would then sneak behind Little Albert, and each time the infant touched the white rat, he would bang a hammer against a steel rod, intentionally frightening the child to the point of tears.

Little Albert grew to fear the rat. He would grow distressed and try to flee from it every time he saw it. Eventually, he was afraid of anything white and furry—even a Santa Claus beard. Watson had succeeded in creating a whole host of irrational fears in an otherwise healthy, normal baby.

Clearly, this experiment was highly unethical and would never be done today, but essentially he proved the power of negative conditioning in humans. We can assume that through fabricated association, we can be conditioned to dislike things because of what they're associated with. You see this a lot with politicians who use smear campaigns against their opponents. In this type of **ad hominem** advertising, they are trying to associate their opponent with something that most people don't like, such as lying, cheating, or irresponsibly spending taxpayer dollars.

Regardless of the legitimacy of such claims, once negative associations have entered the mind, the damage has already been done. In fact, it was reported that even as Little Albert grew older, his phobia of white, furry animals haunted him for the rest of his life. Just like Little Albert, when the public takes hold of a strong negative association, it can sometimes be next to impossible to gain back that confidence. In recent years, we've seen several men and women of great power be stripped of their titles when a small, negative whisper breached the public domain.

Papa John's® CEO and founder, John Schnatter, was a household figure, often times showing up in between the breaks of NFL® games wearing an apron and enjoying pizza with some of the most famous players to ever play the game. However, during the 2017 season, after reportedly making a racist remark during a company earnings call, Schnatter was asked to resign, and Papa John's® ended up losing its sponsorship rights as the official pizza of the NFL®, replaced by Pizza Hut® the next season. A single remark made during a phone call turned the positive Papa John's® figurehead into someone who left a negative taste in the public's mouth for several months.

A few months after Schnatter's departure as CEO, Papa John's® released a new campaign called "Voices" that featured franchisee owners of Papa John's® as the "true voice" of the brand. These real-life restaurant owners showed the world that there was more than one Papa to Papa John's® and that these everyday people were the real backbone to the brand. The campaign did very well, and less than a year after the negative coverage, the company seemed to regain some positive publicity.

Since the whole fiasco, Schnatter has created an entire website devoted to proving his innocence and gives evidence that his former ad agency, Laundry Service®, pressured him into making the remark so they could extort the brand for millions of dollars with the threat of a negative smear campaign. While several sources support Schnatter's claim, the negative association will remain in the public's mind regardless, even if he is later found innocent. This is the strong reality of the new world we live in.

Allegations get front-page press and exonerations rarely get any exposure.

Now, why is it that we are so susceptible to believing associations? The reason is that it often feels like you are the one making the conclusion. Instead of saying something is good or bad, associating them with the respective charge makes the audience believe they have created this label of their own free will. In fact, in the 1960s, Fred Flintstone was shown smoking Winston® cigarettes, smiling and relaxing after a hard day's work in the popular cartoon *The Flintstones*®. With a little repetition of this product placement, some developing minds can begin to form the thought pattern that, "Hey, Fred's doing it. That doesn't seem like a bad thing!" Their impressionable minds can't see that the product has been intentionally positioned to be associated positively.

On the opposite end of the spectrum, the 1990s "Just Say No" campaign negatively associated smoking with life-threatening diseases as an attempt to aid in the US government's "War on Drugs" agenda. Their ads showed a gruesome portrayal of what life is like when a person smokes or takes drugs. The exact same product, used with either a positive or negative association, leads to a much different belief system in the mind of the audience.

Fast-forward to modern day. The cigarette is making a comeback with a rather questionable marketing strategy. Because of the marketing limitations imposed on tobacco companies by the Federal Communications Commission (FCC), most cigarette companies have tightly regulated advertising. However, when Juul® was first introduced they positively associated themselves as a way to quit smoking. They made themselves the solution to cigarette addiction, instead of the problem.

This clever spin on what their product actually was allowed them to not be governed under the typical FCC regulations for cigarettes, in turn, giving them broad exposure to the masses. They later repositioned the product as a recreational e-cigarette, and the product eventually exploded across social media as the New Age cigarette. In January of 2019, Juul® received a $13 billion investment from Altria®, America's largest cigarette company.

Juul® cartridges are currently dominating the marketplace, making up over 70 percent of all national cartridge sales. So, 80 years later, the swing back to cigarettes in American culture was reborn through **cause positioning** and **positive cultural association.**

Now, let's take a look at an elementary school example to see how **emotional sight reading** has become a way for marketers to teach their audiences.

Emotional Sight Reading

When children are learning new words in school, one common technique that teachers use is called **sight reading.** By putting a sticky note with the word "door" on a door, or the word "window" on a window, children can associate the word and the object and learn very quickly.

In a similar fashion, marketers often use this type of technique to condition thoughts about their product by labeling their products with emotion. By advertising an overly happy woman with expensive jewelry, the jeweler is allowing the audience to sight-read "Happy Woman" on the jewelry with no words needed. This elementary technique is put into practice every day, all across the world.

While the ethics behind this technique are rarely ever debated, this covert emotional association technique comes from the same conditioning principles as the Little Albert experiments. Many audiences who are shown these types of ads would probably never come to the conclusion that this is conditioning. However, they can clearly feel the effects of these **manufactured associations** when they begin to create affection for a product.

In the broadcast age, using this technique with repetition performed very well, as consumers would slowly begin to mirror the behavior of the ads with the hope of achieving that emotion. Can you blame them? If an advertiser told us we could buy a unique diamond necklace at half the price of the competition, all while a catchy melody played and a series of beautiful, happy women danced on screen who were we to say otherwise? After all, what evidence could the mind find to debate this ad? Back in the broadcast era, the analog equivalent of research was time-consuming and inefficient, and marketers knew it. It took a lot of work to go store to store to price-check, or to talk to a friend who had purchased the product, or to look up catalogs to try to understand the competitive alternatives to a product.

Before the likes of Google®, Yelp®, and Amazon®, researching a product's credibility or market value was a process that gave marketers a unique advantage. However, in a digitally hyperconnected world, this tactic is no longer as effective. A consumer can instantly summon the reviews of their peers and find out the true story of the product and other options on demand. Audiences can quickly price-check on sites like

Amazon® to see if the product is at a fair market value, making the illusion of an "exclusive product offering" extinct. With a simple Google® search of the item, a host of competitors instantly appear, giving the power of knowledge back to the consumer.

All these factors are a major reason why emotional sight reading and **conditioned association** techniques are becoming antiquated. Consumers now understand that advertising is a game where brands are trying to win the affection of consumers even at the cost of bending the truth or making hollow claims.

Exaggerated associations between product and emotion just don't work with the newer generations because they have an evolved understanding of manufactured storylines. You have to remember modern audiences are magicians. They are now daily content creators on social media, and they too experiment with the tricks of marketing: making a party seem cooler than it is, or acting happy when they really aren't, or making something seem more expensive than it really is. In the same way that it is hard to trick a magician with his own trick, this age-old emotional association illusion is becoming common knowledge, and once the magic is revealed, you can bet classical conditioning won't be fooling the consumers of the future.

Purposive Behaviorism

In the 1950s, psychologist Edward Tolman introduced a new concept that flew directly in the face of classical conditioning. **Purposive behaviorism** proposed that in complex beings, every behavior is aimed at consciously achieving goals.

To demonstrate his theory, Tolman placed three rats in a maze to experiment on their paths of decision-making. For ten days, one rat would receive cheese at the end of the maze. The second rat would receive nothing, and a third rat wouldn't receive anything until the eleventh day, at which point he would receive cheese as well.

After running this test several times, he discovered that the first rat had fewer errors each time he navigated the maze because there was an incentive for him to get to the end as fast as possible. The other rats had no incentive, so they wandered aimlessly through the maze. Tolman observed that the first rat had built a cognitive map of his environment, and even when the starting point was changed, he was still able to find the end of the maze quickly. More interestingly, though, was the third rat, who was given cheese at the end of the maze on the eleventh day. Because he had been exposed to the maze for several days, he had also created a cognitive map of his environment, and when incentivized, he began performing much better than the first rat on its first day receiving the cheese. In addition, when a rat who had eaten a substantial meal was put back into the maze, the rat would often not even complete the maze.

Tolman referred to this concept as **latent learning**. Contrary to the stimulus-response ideas of Pavlov's dog and poor Little Albert, Tolman believed that "**purposeful learning can occur even without actionable evidence.**" While the stimulus-response experiments based their observation on action and reaction, Tolman added that the goal was the key motivator, not the stimulus. If Pavlov had rung a bell for an overly full dog, would the dog still have salivated, or would the satisfaction of its desire change its response?

Tolman theorized that we are constantly shaping our worldview even if we are not perceivably acting on it. The third rat demonstrated that when it had the goal of achieving the maze quickly, it could do so with ease. However, during the first ten days of trial, when the rat's goal of expedited completion was not present, it would wander around the world of the maze. Tolman used this experiment and several others to underscore that **purposive behaviorism is present in all of our actions**, and purpose can trump conditioning. Tolman concluded that **our actions are determined by our motivations to achieve specific goals.**

In advertising today, we are still using the stimulus-response ideology to move consumers to action. But what happens when the purposive mindset of a generation shifts? Will a vegan be seduced to hunger with a juicy hamburger ad? Will an environmentalist find affection for a gas-guzzling sports car in a well-conditioned commercial? Or are the forces of purpose and identity in the minds of consumers affecting their perception of brands in the marketplace? Are we moving to an era where the social and environmental effect of a product will be considered at every purchase? To find out where we are as a society, let's look into the four basic levels of purpose.

The Four Levels of Purpose

The brain is the filter for purpose and is made up of three primary working parts.

1. The first part is the brainstem, which is the lowermost, primal portion of the brain and is used for the most basic functions of the body for survival.
2. The second portion is the cerebellum, which regulates motor skills and emotion.
3. The third part is the cerebrum, which makes up almost 80 percent of the total brain and hosts several processing regions for analyzing logic and cognition.

As a human matures, so does their brain, along with their overall understanding of purpose in the world. A baby lives its early years with the sole purpose of survival and growth. Since the cerebrum is still developing, it does not have the intellectual capacity to consider any greater purpose.

As a child grows older and develops a more mature cerebellum, purpose shifts toward personal fulfillment for needs that are greater than just survival. In the later stages of life, the cerebrum becomes fully developed, and purpose is seen through a more complex web of belief and understanding. It is at this level that our purpose can defy our logic. Let's dive into the specific levels of purpose below.

Purpose Level 1: Survival

At the first level of purpose, our goal is survival—food, water, shelter, and the basic needs. The purpose of our early years is simply to survive. This is the lowest level of purpose and is the foundation for the later levels.

Purpose Level 2: Accumulation

It's not enough to just survive. Evolution rewards individuals who accumulate as much as possible. That's why the second level of purpose is accumulation. We have an innate desire for abundance. Our desire to accumulate is the basis of consumerism. However, this is a rational next step in the development of the ego to accumulate as much as possible because, in some essence, that is an extension of survival. The more one accumulates, the better their chances of survival.

Purpose Level 3: Idealism

The third level of purpose is idealism. This is similar to a concept known as the law of **diminishing marginal utility**. When you get to a certain point— a certain number of dollars in your bank account, a certain amount of food in your cupboard, a bunch of big, fancy things in your big, fancy house—you don't derive much more value from accumulating more. When your desire for accumulation has been satisfied, you step into an idealistic role. How do I want the world to be, and how can I give back?

For whatever reason, some people arrive at this sense of purpose long before they accumulate to the point of saturation. They just make the change. They realize, "All right, this isn't as fulfilling unless I give back to society." Individuals operating on the idealistic level of purpose ask themselves, "What gifts do I have that I can use to make the world a better place?"

Purpose Level 4: Transformation
The final state of purpose is transformative. This is most relevant in religion. In a lot of religions—for example, the concept of enlightenment in Buddhism—you reach a point at which you are no longer trying to attain understanding. You become the *channel* for understanding. If you've gotten to the point that you comprehend it all and can start channeling that understanding, you're just a piece of the fabric of existence. Being at the level of **transformative purpose**, therefore, means you become your purpose.

2.3 What is Brand Purpose?

By now, you might be wondering, what does all this science and psychology have to do with how brands can tell a purpose-told story? Well, here it is.

Classical conditioning is the hallmark of traditional advertising. Brands are quantifying the input and the output: the stimulus and the response. The advertisement is the stimulus, and the response is that consumers buy the product. A brand's sense of purpose, therefore, is derived from accumulation, and if a consumer draws their sense of purpose from the same level, it's an easy sell. They are "Sold on Profit." A for-profit business selling to a for-profit person.

But what happens when an entire generation begins to move from an accumulative purpose to an **idealistic purpose**? These types of messages no longer resonate. The consumer and the business are now at different levels of purpose.

Keep in mind that marketers were the ones who basically invented the culture of consumerism. They built the brands we know and love today by associating the ideals of consumption with happiness. So, while this move may not be a quick one, I think there is plenty of evidence to suggest society has begun the process.

> **Most brands operate purely in the accumulative state. They want to acquire as much profit as possible. But what if they asked the question, "With my strategic offerings and the things that my organization can give the world, how could I make this a better place?" That would move them to a state of idealistic purpose.**

Individuals operating in that idealistic or transformative state will volunteer, give back, and donate to benevolent causes. They'll do things that are actually counterintuitive to accumulation—even counterintuitive to survival. They're depleting their resources for the betterment of others. This is the essence of idealism.

I think the best way to define brand purpose is to explain what it's **not**.

> **Purpose is not the mission, it's not the vision, and it's not the goal. Purpose is the calling.**

Individual purpose is the meaning of existence. The same applies to brand purpose. It's the reason behind why a company does what it does, which is essential to the direction of your business. When you're living with purpose, what you do becomes the tangible equivalent of why you do it.

If you're living with a goal, the environment may change, so the goal may also change. A lot of times, even your vision may change direction if the market's not ready, but **your purpose never changes.** Purpose should be the one thing that is constant throughout—it is the higher meaning that perseveres no matter what happens in the marketplace. The purpose always remains the same.

> **Purpose is the role we were ultimately meant to play in the world.**

Why Brands Must Adopt a Transformative, Purpose-Driven Mindset

In a meaningful brand that utilizes purpose-driven advertising, the input is belief and idea-making. The output is not the transaction, but a state of understanding.

> **In purpose-driven advertising, brands don't create a call to action. They create a call to belief.**

We know that great brands can be a catalyst for change, but once they've catalyzed change, they can also become the engine for that to continue. That is the transformative level of purpose.

If a brand gets to the state of transformation, it's no longer trying to change the world. It is becoming a fabric of what the world needs. It is in the ecosystem of purpose. It creates alignment with consumers who identify with what your brand stands for, and, over time, that alignment turns into brand loyalty.

When Coke® enters developing countries, they often pay the costs needed to develop essential parts of the supply chain like roads and infrastructure. This infrastructure then gets used for mobility and further development of the native people, which leads to greater opportunities for them all around the world. This is the idea of being in the transformative level of purpose. A brand becomes the path to opportunity for humanity and is rewarded by consumers with their loyalty. Recently, there has been a movement to focus brands toward this greater level of purpose by acknowledging their responsible action in a certification called B Corp. This B Corp. status tells consumers that these companies operate with a higher purpose and are responsible with their actions.

As we discussed before, traditional marketing is like a stimulus-response experiment. It's giving the stimulus and expecting the response right away. It's ringing a bell and hoping the consumer starts to drool. But with purposive behaviorism, brands aim to create a worldview. Just like Tolman's latent learning effect, the brand is advertising a belief, and those who believe it will, in the end, buy into the brand, not just the product.

Clarity of Purpose

A lot of organizations struggle to answer the question, "Why do we do what we do?" Their mission statements are clunky, the message is overwhelming, and it's not really clear what they actually are out there to do. At best, they offer very ambiguous statements for what the organization does, but rarely any mention of why they do it. And the bigger the organization, the more ambiguous it is.

Any statement regarding purpose almost gets lost in translation. You hear these things like "vision" and "mission," but what's the purpose? That's never talked about in the boardroom. The very first step is to create **clarity of purpose.**

> **Definiteness of purpose is the starting point of all achievement.**

I talk more in-depth about clarity of purpose in Chapter 4: Finding Brand Purpose. Clarity of purpose is important because **it gives meaning to every department.** Across the board—especially if you're a multi-disciplined organization and offer a lot of different products and services—it is so empowering when you have one meaningful, clearly defined purpose that ties everything together.

If you're a staunch traditionalist, it's possible that you've read this far and still aren't convinced in the power of the purpose-told story. In the next chapter, we'll dive into an objective understanding of what "inspiration" is in the purpose-story, and we'll take a look at the ecosystem of the **purpose economy.** We'll also examine some case studies that prove that purpose-driven marketing is here to stay.

Chapter 3:

The Age of Purpose

In an article for PRWeek Magazine®, Jae Goodman, CEO of Observatory, said,

> **We're finally at that inflection point I thought was going to happen ten years ago. It is irrefutable at this point—data, not just instinct, supports it.... Marketers cannot justify dumping all of that investment into performance and promotion. There has to be a reinvestment in brand storytelling.**

Brands are starting to see the metrics proving that the old vanity marketing of the past—being the best, the shiniest, the fastest, the whatever—is no longer resonating. They now need to tell meaningful **brand storytelling** about who they are and what they believe in. This is compelling evidence to many marketers that the marketplace is beginning to make a shift.

Let's take a look at some of the most recent eras we have graduated from below.

- The Digital Age: technology empowered innovation on a large scale and made modern communication tools available to the masses

- The Information Age: information became omnipresent and freely available to everyone on the internet
- The Participation Age: consumers could now participate in the global conversation by creating content for blogs, social media, Wikipedia, consumer ratings, etc.

Now, in an information-rich, hyper connected world, consumers are so saturated with data and so connected with their peers that they are beginning to feel a lack of meaning and real connection.

Consumers are no longer seeking information, they are seeking substance. They are starving for authenticity. They are seeking the real stories of purpose. This is the onset to the age of purpose.

Marry Your Customer

The old model of heavily promoting products to drive transactions is a game of catch and release. If you amplify an advertisement enough, you will get a response, but in the absence of this stimulus, the response rate decreases dramatically.

Traditional marketing is like a one night stand. You are engaging in a relationship purely for the end transaction; the lifetime value of the relationship means little to nothing.

Purpose-driven marketing, on the other hand, is all about lifetime value. It's more like looking for your life companion. You're seeking the right connection at the right time to the right person. If you play all your cards right, on the first encounter, you might get a second date. And if you prove yourself on the second date, you could start a relationship.

The desire for the sale in purpose-driven marketing comes secondary to the desire for the relationship. Therefore, the mindset of the process changes from value extraction to value addition.

Think about the process you go through when courting a companion. You spend time and money. You provide value and insight. You give much more than you take, and in return for all this, you receive loyalty. Had you skipped the previous steps and asked for loyalty, it would have never worked out. Or, if your only objective was purely transactional, the long-term relationship would have very little depth and would likely not succeed. You need to give to your consumers first.

Afterall, why date your customers when you can marry them?

3.1 Inspiration; the Double Helix; and the Business of Goosebumps

The word "inspiration" comes from the Latin word *inspirati*, which means "to fill with life," or, in some translations, "to fill thyself."

A lot of people use the words "motivation" and "inspiration" interchangeably, but the key difference is that motivation is an inner push while inspiration is an inner pull. Motivation pushes you to who you want to become; inspiration pulls you to who you really are. I've met tons of people who are motivated to be healthy. They start a New Year's diet, look in the mirror, and say, "All right, I'm doing this! I'm going to the gym! I *want* to get in the best shape of my life!"

Five weeks later, they cancel their gym membership and are back to their normal routine. The reason is, people who are motivated to be healthy probably don't really want to go to the gym or eat healthy. Their motivation is nothing more than a fabricated desire so they can achieve the outcome of being healthy. They want the outcome, not the journey.

On the other hand, I do know people who are truly inspired to be healthy. A good friend of mine, Mark Lauren, has devoted his entire life to being a personal trainer and nutritionist. He's written books and created workout DVDs. He travels the world and teaches some of the top Navy SEALs how to get in the best shape of their lives. One time, he even swam underwater for over two and a half minutes during a special operation class all the way to the point of unconsciousness to really push his body to the limit. You know why? Because he is inspired to be healthy. He doesn't just want the outcome. He wants the whole journey and the lifestyle. When I get around this guy, I think, "Does this dude ever think about anything other than working out and eating healthy?" It's easy to see that he's ascended far beyond motivation and into the realm of inspiration.

Motivation wears off with time, but inspiration, once it gets sparked, continues to grow.

People who are inspired are powerful, even dangerous people. They'll run until they pass out and study until they fall asleep. Inspired people are almost always people who have found their purpose. They've literally found something in their life that, the more energy they pour into it, the more energy they get out. Now that's inspiring!

The Staircase that Changed the World

On the campus of the University of Cambridge, there is a popular tale about an architect and a scientist that has been told for decades. In the early 1950s, a young architect at Cambridge was finishing his graduate degree in architecture and, as a passion project, proposed to build a spiral staircase on campus. Since the university had no immediate need, they told him to build it in the commons if he wished, but it would be nothing more than a temporary art display.

And so, the architect designed and erected a fifteen-foot spiral staircase to nowhere. It sat there for several weeks. There was no real reason behind it other than the fact that he was passionate about his craft and had been inspired to build it. During that time, a research scientist came along named Dr. James D. Watson. Watson had been toiling to discover the composition of DNA for several years, and although he knew what elements made up DNA, he simply could not figure out how the structure was formulated.

One day, while walking across the university campus, Watson sat at the base of the spiral staircase art installation. As Dr. Watson began to eat his lunch, he froze in mid-bite and suddenly had the eureka moment. A spiraling double helix! It explained how all the pieces were connected. DNA was a spiraling double helix. Looking at the staircase, he pieced together in his mind how all the elements would connect. And he was right.

Watson and his colleague, Crick, soon published the first description of DNA's double helix structure—the genetic code that makes up all life as we know it. This discovery changed the entire field of genetics, as well as our understanding of the living world. It even earned Watson and Crick the Nobel Prize in 1962. But what about the architect?

No one will ever know who the architect was that inspired Watson's revelation. He won't go down as a famous name in the history books and may have never even known that he was responsible for such an important moment in time … but that's okay.

This architect's purpose wasn't to change the world. But he inspired a man who would. That was his role in the world. His passion to create the staircase gave way to a discovery that is still today responsible for more cures and more new medicine than any other genetic discovery.

The point is, when we are inspired toward a purpose, it can also inspire others to their purpose. That's because inspiration is extremely contagious. Anytime you're around someone who is truly inspired, it is infectious. Even though the architect and Dr. Watson never met, their connection will live on forever.

Now think about your brand. Are you the scientist or the architect? Are you saving the world or inspiring your consumers to do so? Can your brand be purposeful and inspire your consumers to do the same? How do you know when you are really inspiring your audience? Let's jump into what it feels like to be inspired by an idea.

The Business of Goosebumps

You can feel inspiration. Intuitively, we all know when we are passionately compelled toward something or truly inspired. Many people associate the feeling of inspiration with goosebumps or chills throughout the body. It's as if they are tapping into their true purpose or feeling some sort of divine attraction.

The truth is, all mammals get goosebumps. The technical term is **piloerection**. The muscles underneath the hair follicles contract, and your hairs go up. At its most fundamental level, goosebumps are a means of survival triggered by the fight-or-flight response. For a mammal covered in hair, a piloerection makes the creature appear bigger and more intimidating than it really is. That's why if you're petting a dog and the fur on the back of its neck stands up, you know you should probably stop petting it. He's having a fight-or-flight response. His body is telling him, "This could be a meaningful moment of survival." Also, when mammals encounter frigid temperatures, piloerection creates a fluffier, more insulating layer of fur to protect the body from the cold. In both cases, you can see that goosebumps, or "the chills," are about survival.

Humans, however, have evolved to the point that goosebumps can be an indication of a meaningful, rich moment. They can be a sign that your instinct and your logic are in full agreement. You may have listened to a motivational speaker before or watched a heartwarming movie when, all of a sudden, you feel this overwhelming sensation of goosebumps. Logically and physiologically, you are experiencing a rush of insight where your body is having a strong emotional reaction to the sensation of meaning.

As marketers in the age of purpose, we are all in the business of goosebumps.

There are millions of videos, photos, and blogs out there that your audience consumes daily. It's your job to make sure that when they are consuming your brand's content, you give them the goosebumps. One of the best ways to do this is with the purpose-told story.

For years, I admired the P&G® ads that would air on Mother's Day depicting a heartwarming story of moms being the humble heroes of the house. Picking up toys after their kids would go to sleep, cleaning the dishes in the late hours of the night, and doing laundry before the rest of the house wakes up. These ads would give me goosebumps every time because they connected me with the feelings I had about my mom as a kid. At the end of the commercial, their slogan would simply read "P&G®: The Proud Sponsor of Moms." No product or promotion or 1-800 number. Just a simple call to belief that would resonate with anyone.

While this may sound like a foolish marketing strategy in traditional advertising, P&G® is creating a strong emotional connection with moms through stories like this, which paint their key consumer as the hero. Just like the empowerment marketing model and the orientation effect we discussed earlier in the book, this strategy allows the brand to earn brand loyalty in the mind of the consumers because it reinforces that the brand and the consumer share the same beliefs. By showing those empowering moments of truth, your brand can inspire its consumers.

Frisson and ASMR

Autonomous sensory meridian response (ASMR) is an experience characterized by a static-like tingling sensation on the skin that typically begins at the scalp and moves down the back of the neck and upper spine. I'm sure you've felt this feeling before. It's the "chills" that run from your neck down your upper back when you experience something emotionally provoking. It's typically a very pleasurable experience. Some people even refer to it as a "skin orgasm." It's also a strong sign that a great story is stimulating the body.

Today, if you search online, you will find a whole community of people who call themselves "ASMRtists." They are commonly audio bloggers who use highly stimulating sounds like ice cubes gently stirring in a glass drink or fingernails tapping on a concrete surface to induce ASMR. What they have discovered is that by using an auditory or visual stimulus, or a combination of the two, we can synthetically create a feeling in the body that is often associated with that of empowerment or inspiration, which is rather fascinating.

In addition to ASMR, **"frisson"** is another psychophysiological response that can be induced through video. While ASMR is centralized to the upper back, frisson is a quick onset of piloerections that fly across different sections of the body like the arms or legs. What is important about these two reactions is that they are the body's way of validating that what you are watching is meaningful.

While both responses can be brought on by an incredible story, they are more likely the result of the delivery of the story. For example, a slowly building, inspirational orchestral track with a child whispering a message will have a much greater chance of eliciting this response than the same message yelled during a fast hard rock music bed.

The delivery of your purpose story is important as you consider these two reactions because you are setting the tone of what type of response you want to receive. With the amount of noise in the marketplace right now, differentiating your brand through a feeling can be a remarkable way to retain and grow your audience, and, based on what we are learning about the induction of ASMR and frisson, the delivery of your story can be just as important as the story itself.

3.2 Purpose Over Product

All this might sound great from a motivational standpoint, but you're probably wondering where profit fits into the equation.

> The scary truth is that a business whose sole purpose is profit will not thrive in the new economy, regardless of how good their product is. In an information-rich world, consumers will perceive the corporate accumulation of wealth as a vehicle for division if it does not have a social counterpart.

With transparency at an all-time high, brands are pants down, streaking across the global stage, constantly in the crossfire of public opinion. We've seen it with the NFL's® position on kneeling during the National Anthem and a string of major corporations like Uber® dealing with sexual harassment and inclusion issues. Incidents that might have been swept under the rug twenty years ago now significantly impact consumer behavior, from patriotic groups blacking out NFL® games to 200,000 deleted Uber® accounts during the #DeleteUber movement. With minute-by-minute reporter tweets, in-depth consumer product reviews, and viral social media rants, people are waging campaigns against brands instead of the other way around (more on this in Chapter 8).

In this collective society, consumers have become the strongest influencers of their own perceptions. The key point that brands must acknowledge in the new marketplace is that the world is judging them far beyond their product. They are judging brands on their process and authenticity of purpose.

We are all storytellers. Not everybody writes them down, of course, but there's always a story to tell: how you got your job, your all-time worst date, that crazy thing that happened at the store, the excuse you give if you're late to the office, a storm in Texas, a mission trip to the Dominican Republic.... Stories are all around us.

We've come a long way from eagerly waiting for the next book hot off the printing press. There's now an unending stream of drama, comedy, news, and reality TV. Each day, social media channels give play-by-play analyses of life, and streaming services are supplying full seasons of new content every single day. We are swimming in a sea of stories, most of which have little to no substance. But what if we could get back to great storytelling?

As master storyteller Robert McKee once said, "Stories are the fabric of understanding; they give evidence to the pattern of life." It is through stories that we understand the world and our relationship to it. We all live in a way that fits the logic of the stories we've been told. In many ways, we behave in the way stories have told us to behave.

Culture is built on the principle of imitation. We demonstrate the normality of life and human behavior through the stories we perpetuate.

In the same way a parent teaches a baby to clap by demonstrating a clap, our culture is built on stories that we have grown up to **imitate.** "Monkey see, monkey do" is the mantra of the new generation who are learning life via social media and YouTube®. The hyper-accessibility to great stories and information makes telling a truly unique and compelling story even harder.

So why is it so hard for brands to tell effective stories? The main reason is that the motive of most business stories is to sell. This is an old way of thinking that is still lingering from the broadcast age. When marketers were paying hundreds of thousands for broadcast airtime and radio commercials, it made sense that they would cut right to the chase and go straight for the sale, but the distribution channels now have dynamically changed. Today, it cost nothing to host great story-driven videos on social media or build a high-quality podcast worth listening to.

> **The opportunity to tell great stories is at an all-time high, but for these stories to be truly effective, they must be art, not ads.**

Our audience is understandably skeptical about the stories we tell. In fact, if anything even remotely sounds like an ad or marketing material, there's an immediate red flag in the viewer's mind: "Warning! I am being sold. I am being manipulated!"

In the new age of storytelling, brands have some rehabilitation to go through. They must regain the trust of their audience. Brands can't just say something anymore. They have to act upon their purpose and their values. Doing so shows an audience what they really believe.

Purpose, therefore, is the driver of all action. If you say your purpose is to help the environment but you do the opposite, you have created a gap. If there are incongruities between your words and your actions, it will be evident to all of your consumers. This will deter consumers from buying into your brand far more than producing a bad product ever could.

Life's Calling

The purpose-told story is a long-term strategy. If you find yourself wondering where to begin or if your brand should even bother, let's think about what it's like when a person discovers his or her purpose on an individual level.

There comes a time in your life when you look in the mirror and realize that what you see is all you will ever be. You're not growing any taller. You're not getting any younger. The only way to give clear direction to all your decision-making and to make the most out of your time in this life is to pinpoint your true purpose.

> The search for your true purpose will be most success-
> ful when you have an objective internal and external
> perspective of your meaning in the world. Purpose is
> our meaning for existence—your atlas for all action.

It can be frustrating trying to find your purpose. It's like looking at the same reflection over and over again and trying to see a new image. You may find yourself in a spiral of critical doubt. The idea of doing some introspective excavation to find purpose by asking hypothetical questions may feel like an eternal rhetorical exercise, but nobody ever found buried treasure just by looking at the map. You have to get your shovel dirty.

One challenge is that you cannot physically be outside your own body. Things about yourself that might seem obvious to others could take you years to discover. When it comes to finding your brand's purpose, however, this is the greatest advantage you could ask for. You operate from the perspective of the brand, of course, but you also have the ability to see things from the point of view of the passive observer of the brand: you can view your brand as its audience.

The Desire Audit

Many people *think* they know what their purpose is until you ask them to define it. Then you'll hear them give some long-winded, ambiguous, idealistic image of how the world should be. Why is it so hard to define purpose in a single sentence?

While studying the process of finding purpose, I came across several self-help books that more or less had the exact same antidote for discovery, and that was the desire audit—an introspective dig into the things you inherently desire. It's a very simple process, which is probably why it's so popular. It goes a little something like this.

1. Think about the thing you are most passionate about. Your deepest desire. The thing that you would do all day long if you had enough money that you didn't have to work.
2. Think of a way to make that your occupation so you can spend the majority of your life getting paid to do what you love.
3. Repeatedly tell yourself that this is your purpose.

Voila. You've figured it out. However.....

The problem I have with this process is that it leads to *fulfillment*, not purpose. Fulfillment is feeling good about what you do, while living your purpose is actually being what you were meant to be. Fulfillment is the end feeling, and purpose is the reason.

So how can your brand discover its purpose? Let's take a look.

Chapter 4:

Finding Brand Purpose

Finding your brand's purpose is no easy task. I spent weeks trying to read all the self-help books and quick-fix blogs I could find about brand purpose, and they all failed to mention one critical issue with brand purpose. It's an issue I've seen over and over again: **You don't actually "find" your brand's purpose.**

"Finding your purpose" is a figure of speech that is used in this book and all over the world to label the event that is typically a personal discovery. However, we are talking about brands, not people, and that's rarely how the discovery of a brand's purpose happens. In fact, if you look deep into the context in which great brands have "found" their purpose, you will find that, more often than not, they were simply at the right vantage point to see clearly what was right in front of them all along.

In this chapter, we'll break down the unique vantage point by which we can best see your brand's purpose and how to put it into a meaningful expression.

4.1 Meaning-Making

As we discussed previously, humans are cerebral creatures and descendants of primal hunter-gatherers. It is a mechanism of our own survival to take data and make meaning out of it. For example, let's say we are hunting with our tribe in the forest and hear a tree branch rustle and a loud rumble in the distance. We take those two meaningless data points and, by instinct, instantly create meaning in our mind. Think to yourself for a second what these two noises may mean.

Perhaps we believe that the rustle in the branch could mean there is a predator approaching or a herd is stampeding. Or maybe we believe that a storm is creeping in and the wind rustling the branches is foreshadowing its arrival. The simple observation of the moving tree branch and the rumble in the distance is useless to us until we apply our own meaning. It's highly possible that you could have thought these two events meant something completely different.

The point here is that adding experience or a learned association to an observation is how we create meaning, and when meaning is applied back to the observation, it gives insight to action. Based on what we perceive the meaning of those two events to be, will influence how we act in response to them. But the single biggest variable to responsive action is not just how we interpret the meaning; rather, it's our core intent of the outcome.

Finding our core intention in life provides clarity to purpose because it indicates which of the four stages of purpose we are currently in, which determines the meaning of our own actions (survival, accumulation, idealistic, transformative). But before we discuss core intent, let's dive deeper into perceiving the meaning of our own purpose.

The Purpose Conundrum

If our minds are literally programmed to find meaning in everything in life, and the most basic meaning is our purpose in the world, why is it so difficult to just find our purpose? The problem is in what I call the **purpose conundrum.** The purpose conundrum describes the difficulty in perspective of being both the observer and the observed. The distorted state of both *being* you and *searching for* you complicates the discovery process.

Physics tells us that an object cannot be an object to itself. Water can't wet itself, fire can't burn itself, and light can't illuminate itself. Likewise, you can't just find yourself. For example, if you were to take your eye and turn it as far as you could and try to focus as near as possible, you would still never be able to physically see your own eye. That is because an eye cannot see itself. However, by changing your perspective and looking outward to a mirror, the eye can see itself clearly through the reflection.

> **Today, we are going cross-eyed as a culture, trying to find our purpose from the introspective vantage point of our own perspective.**

Focus Questions

I believe brands need to look outward, like an eye gazing into a mirror, to really find themselves. Tell your executive team for just a moment to abandon the inward focus of vision, assets, positioning, mission, etc., and turn their eyes toward the bigger outward picture. Look past your product for just one moment and into the broader portrait of your consumers and their families and their towns and their world. Ask yourself:

1. Gift question: "What is the unique gift my brand can give to the world?"
2. Desire question: "What is the problem we want to solve?"
3. Opportunity question: "Where is the opportunity to do this?"

This is a much more comprehensive look into your brand in relation to the world because it reveals what you can do, what you want to do, and where you have an opportunity to do it.

Most brands' purpose relates to the opportunity that is closest to them. For example, Coca Cola's® purpose, "to refresh the world in mind, body and spirit," has a familiar ring to their product offering while stating the three focus area of how they plan to make the world better. Since 1984, the company has spent almost $1 billion on causes prioritizing women's empowerment, access to clean drinking water, and the development of disadvantaged youth. Other companies like Adidas®, who have a purpose of changing lives through the power of sports, leverage their sports apparel sales to give back to disadvantaged countries. Adidas® even pledged to make over 5 million shoes in reclaimed plastics from the ocean. Whole Foods®, Subway®, Merk®, Novartis®—all have purposes that relate to helping the world be healthier, and they demonstrate strong corporate responsibility initiatives that support their purpose.

Chances are, your brand purpose is likely much closer than you think. Your industry and location are unique to your brand, so those are things you should really consider when you are creating your statement of purpose.

Critical Focus

Moving through life is like a camera constantly changing lenses. When you are young, you see the world through a wide-angle lens. It appears very big, and the possibilities are endless. As you grow older, you begin to zoom in and focus more on the future. You begin to act for tomorrow as well as today. Over time, your view becomes narrower and narrower as your foreseeable possibilities come into focus. While this is essential for progression, the problem with this process is that as we gain clarity on who we are *becoming*, we can lose focus on who we really are.

In photography, this effect is called "exceeding critical focus." If you are using a long zoom lens and an object is close enough to the lens, the camera literally will not see it. The light will bend around the object, and whatever is in distant focus will not be obstructed. You could hold a pencil right in front of the lens, and in the final image, you would never know it was there.

That's the situation many brands are in today. Over time, they have narrowed their focus so keenly on what they do that they have lost focus of why they do it. When they try to find their purpose, they realize that the thing that is closest to them is the hardest to see. It's hidden in plain sight.

Now, imagine again for a moment that you are the camera looking into the mirror. As you are looking through the lens, you are also looking back at yourself. From this perspective, it's obvious what was right in front of you this whole time. From this reflection, you can perceive yourself from the outside, so you can see both yourself and the world in the background. In fact, you are now perceiving the brand from the vantage point at which the world sees it.

By answering the three focus questions in the previous section and looking at your brand with the world in the backdrop, hopefully this will help provide the vantage point to understand the unique opportunity of purpose for your brand.

Come to the quiet point of understanding that your company cannot be all things to all people. Clarity of purpose is far greater than scale of purpose.

Many corporations aim to do all things good and end up confusing the marketplace on who they are. Being generally good is not enough. Clarity and conciseness are key. In the same way that you can't boil the ocean, you can't be good all around. But the more finite your purpose is, the easier it is to understand your true meaning.

Harley Davidson's® purpose is to help people find personal freedom. Simple and straight to the point. Apple's® purpose is to challenge the status quo. Again, simple and straightforward.

Word choice becomes extremely important here. If you are going to express this to people, you need to have no ifs, ands, or buts. It's got to be *exactly* what you mean. My company's purpose is to inspire people through video. And if I'm telling someone this for the first time, it becomes crucial that I clearly define what *inspiration* means to me, because I don't want to be vague or to assume that they define it the same way.

Choose Your Stage

Another helpful tool in pinpointing brand purpose starts with defining our stage of purpose. In the example of hunting in the forest, it is assumed that the main purpose is **Survival** (the first stage of purpose), so our action would be one that best fits that purpose, like finding shelter from the storm or running from an oncoming predator. However, if we are in the second stage of purpose, **Accumulation**, the action may be to gather first, *then* run.

While it seems like a crazy idea that someone would pursue accumulation over survival, it happens quite often in business. In fact, in Japan, this has become a widespread epidemic. Many salarymen in the cities work 80-plus-hour workweeks to try to build their status, only to die in their early thirties from over-exhaustion. In the 1970s, the Japanese government even coined a term for this, *karoshi*, which translates to "overwork death," for the thousands of workers who were dying prematurely from sheer exhaustion. This phenomenon of focusing on wealth over health is prevalent in all parts of the world. By the same token, when a brand pursues a purpose of accumulation over survival, putting profit over people, it may experience some incredible short-term gains, but in the long term, it is setting the stage for a premature death.

Look at the case of Bernie Madoff, who pulled off the largest Ponzi scheme in the history of the stock market. His purpose was massive accumulation. In the early 2000s, Madoff defrauded his clients for an estimated $65 billion and, even up until the very week of his arrest in 2008, was reportedly still trading stocks to earn his way out.

Madoff prioritized the accumulation of wealth over his very well-being. Knowing that the threat of being caught was at an all-time high, Madoff could have easily "made off." He had the money and resources to flee town. However, he was still trying to accumulate more on the very week of his arrest. So, while we say it would be crazy for a person or a brand to pursue the purpose of accumulation over the purpose of survival, it happens more often than you may think.

As we discussed before, the third stage of purpose is **Idealism**. In the forest example, if we are acting based on an idealistic purpose, we may act as the hero and take it upon ourselves to fight off the lurking predator or help others escape the storm before helping ourselves. If a storm is approaching, we might build a shelter for the young, etc. This stage is all about thinking of others over yourself. And if we are in the fourth stage of purpose, **Transformative**, we have a deep understanding of our role at this moment.

We understand the role of the predator and the storm, and we know the purpose of the event, as well as the exact action we should take. The fourth stage is almost impossible to attain for people, but for a brand, it is quite possible.

For the sake of this book, let's assume your brand is seeking the third stage of purpose: Idealism. Defining your stage of purpose will give you an even more comprehensive understanding of your purpose while you are trying to define it. It simply allows for the parameters of possibility so that you can more easily narrow in on your main purpose.

Describing Value – The Levels of Purpose

Marketing is essentially the process of describing value. You describe value across three main areas: what, how, and why.

What is your product? Categorically, what do you do? This is the easiest part to describe. It's the way that most companies describe what they do. The Solo Cup Company®, for instance, provides a container to drink out of. It's just what they do.

How is it produced? What is the process for creating your product? You might look at some other cup competitors and say, "Well, their cups are organic/biodegradable/environmentally friendly." This second level of description is particularly important to consumers nowadays.

Why does it exist? The deepest level of the description is to describe why. This is a core belief. For example, "We want to help the world drink better." By branding in a bright green cup and promising to use a portion of your profits to create wells in Africa, you have now added a meaningful value proposition to your marketing mix. Consumers can buy any cup—they are basically all the same—but the fact that your cup has a "Why" now elevates it from a commodity to a cause.

Lance Armstrong's Livestrong Foundation® sold millions of Livestrong® wristbands on this same idea, with proceeds from sales supporting people affected by cancer. You could buy a bracelet anywhere, but the Livestrong® wristband wasn't just a bracelet; it was a symbol that you supported a greater cause. It wasn't a fashion statement. It was a belief statement.

For many years, belief statements didn't matter. Consumers were buying *what*. *How* didn't really mean much. And *why* was so far from people's minds that it was almost trivial. But purpose is exceedingly important nowadays. It is one of the only means by which you can differentiate on a substantial level. Competitors may have the same materials, do the same things, and follow the same process, but their *why* may be totally different. JW Marriott® is a great example of this. They have a lot of competitors; the hotel market is just saturated. But they have a distinct advantage: a very interesting brand story.

JW Marriott® started out as a nine-stool root beer stand. John Willard Marriott had a stand he would cart around personally, where you could sit down and have a root beer with your friends. He became so successful with his stand that he started a restaurant. The restaurant had such incredible food that he became one of the largest providers of airline food. From there, he decided to get into the hotel business because he wanted to create an environment that was a meaningful place for people to stay while out of town.

You look at that story, and it's so unique. Hilton® doesn't have that story. Hyatt® doesn't have that story. No one other than Marriott® can have that story. If you try to differentiate a hotel chain based on the *what* factor, you really can't. If you try to differentiate on *how*, there are still a lot of similarities there. But if you differentiate based on *why*, that's where things can be completely different. That's the idea behind describing your unique story in the marketplace. The value is no longer on exterior things. It's on the interior.

Self-Evaluation – Levels of Awareness

Years ago, I heard an old limerick from British philosopher Alan Watts that stuck with me. It goes:

> There once was a man who said so,
> It seems that I know that I know,
> but I'd sure like to see
> the eye who sees me,
> so I know that I know that I know.

I always loved the way this sounded, but it wasn't until recently that I suddenly came to understand its greater meaning. It's the critical focus analogy all over again but on a far larger scale.

As humans, we are aware of our present moment. In your case, you are aware that you are reading. This is biological awareness. But what's even more fascinating about our species is that we have a second level of awareness. We, therefore, are **aware of our awareness.** In the philosophical/anthropological sense, we possess consciousness of consciousness; not only can you read a book and digest its words into meaning, but you are aware that the experience of reading is happening and can self-evaluate the greater purpose of the event.

At this second level of awareness, you can even wander into other thoughts while still in the first level of awareness. Many daily commuters know this feeling all too well. They consciously drive to work each day but find themselves vividly daydreaming about unrelated thoughts. At the first level of awareness, you **do.** At the second level, you **perceive.** But only at the third level—the perspective of an outsider existing beyond yourself—can you truly **understand.** That's when "you know that you know that you know."

The third state of awareness represents meaning and insight. At the first two levels of awareness, you have the cognitive bias of being both the doer and the perceiver. Third-level observation occurs outside the body and mind, bestowing a sense of detached understanding.

Your advantage is that you can externally perceive your brand. All marketers nowadays are both marketers and consumers. Therefore, you live at this third level of awareness. You can see the brand in relation to the world.

As I stated before, your brand purpose is the meaning for the brand's existence. It isn't its personality or beliefs or values. Discovering purpose is finding what you should be; and realizing who you already are. It's observing the relationship between the brand and the world and understanding the reason for the brand in the universal ecosystem.

Now, as we approach the process of making a strategic brand narrative, let's dive into a few more questions.

Here are some fundamental questions to consider regarding your brand.

1. *What is the unique strength that your organization has?*
2. *What is the moral imperative that the organization abides by?*
3. *What fuels your organization's passion?*
4. *Why does the world need your organization?*
5. *What does your organization aspire to be in the future?*
6. *How do you integrate your core values into your product?*

Now, you need a **Strategic Brand Narrative** that is in line with this purpose.

4.2 The Purpose Story

Your brand's "purpose story" is the strategic brand narrative. This is distinct from a purpose statement in that the purpose story gives evidence for, and lends relevance to, your purpose statement.

In my personal experience, when I tell an audience or prospective client my purpose story *before* I tell them my purpose statement, everything makes sense.

> **Think of your purpose statement as the crescendo to your purpose story.**

No matter how great the song, if you hit the crescendo right away, it feels awkward and abrupt, but a slow build can render a listener awestruck. A slow build in an authentic purpose story allows the purpose statement to feel like a grand finale, ultimately becoming the moral lesson to the story.

A good purpose story is a dynamic journey recounting the highs and lows that have catalyzed your brand. Think about the introduction to this book. If I had come right out and told you, "My purpose is to inspire people through video," it would have sounded like any other purpose statement out there: meaningless and contrived. By sharing the context of my personal life experience—the story that led me to this discovery—and allowing you to share in the moments along the way that sparked my passion, I allowed you to come to your own conclusion. By the end of that story, you already knew my purpose statement. I didn't even have to say it.

Director and storyteller Andrew Stanton of Pixar® calls this "the Unifying Theory of 2+2." Audiences *want* to figure things out for themselves. So let them do the math. Don't give them 4. Give them 2 and 2.

The Value of Perception

Influencing **perceived value** is a major advantage to a strong purpose story. It has the ability to genuinely affect consumers' understanding of value.

Perceived value is the cross section of worth and opinion. Opinion is based largely on an individual's emotionally charged memories of the past. When consumers truly empathize with your brand's purpose story, they are positively charging an emotional record of your story in their memories. Depending on the intensity and repetition of this charge, the consumer is consciously forming and reforming their opinion of your brand.

For example, if you have a painting of a famous artist, even if it's just a stroke on a canvas, it could be worth $50, or $50,000, or $50 million. It is a perceived value. Its worth is not based on the physical value of the paint or the canvas but on the emotional value of what the painting represents. That is how we should look at brand stories—not in the physical sense of the information or product proposition but on the level of emotion, influencing perceived value of your brand in the consumer's mind.

A lot of people think of Pablo Picasso solely as an abstract artist, but he also happened to be an exceptional portrait artist. There's a story about Picasso—possibly apocryphal, but a good story nonetheless—that demonstrates the power of perceived value. One day, after Picasso was already famous, he was in a marketplace when a lady recognized him and asked him to draw a portrait of her. Picasso said, "Oh, sure. I'll do it right now." In about thirty seconds, he sketched a beautiful, realistic portrait. As he handed it over to this lady, he said, "That'll be $20,000."

This woman, stunned nearly beyond words, said, "$20,000? But it took you thirty seconds!"

"No, it didn't," Picasso replied. "It took me thirty years to be able to do that in thirty seconds."

The idea here is that value isn't in the product or the process. It's the perception! To her, the painting was just a small moment of his time; however, to Picasso that moment was an accumulation of years dedicated to training. The way you affect the perception of value, on the very deepest level, is through purpose. So let's break this down.

Why is a thirty-second sketch by Picasso worth $20,000? Because there's a high demand for his work. Why is there a high demand for his work? Because people are attracted to him. Why are people attracted to him? Because his art moves them. Why does his art move them? Because his art has deep meaning to it.

Pretty pictures and pieces of interesting artwork sell every day at Goodwill for about twenty-five cents a-piece. Some of them might even be better-looking than some of Picasso's work, but nobody's spending thousands of dollars on them. Time and time again, value always comes back to purpose.

Where to Share Your Purpose

A few years ago, there was a garage sale in New York where a man bought a $3.00 antique bowl. After a few months of it collecting dust, he decided to take it to an auctioneer to have it appraised. Upon examining the bowl, the auctioneer concluded that it dated back to eighteenth-century China. It turned out it would have been used by the royal family. The auctioneer suggested that it could be worth up to $100,000 if he sold it at a European auction with its story of origin. The man took the auctioneer's advice and listed it in a high-end European auction. In less than two hours, the bowl sold for $2.8 million.

At the garage sale, the bowl was practically worthless. In the home of the new owner, the bowl still had little value. To the educated auctioneer, the bowl was worth thousands— maybe even $100,000. But in the final auction, paired with a compelling backstory, it was worth millions. The bowl never changed. The story was what made all the difference. This is also an important lesson about how **the environment in which we tell our purpose story** can change its effect on perceived value.

In the same likeness, selling peanuts at a baseball game isn't a great venue to explain the origin story of the nuts, the passion of the brand's founder, or how the sale affects humanity by providing jobs to underprivileged kids in India. Some marketplaces, like a baseball game or a garage sale, are purely transactional. They have little volatility when it comes to perceived value. However, in the right setting, like the high-end auction, with a captive audience and a compelling story of your purpose, the entire value proposition increases.

By projecting your purpose into a marketplace where consumers have a discretionary income and giving them a meaningful reason for why your product is helping save lives or helping the earth or making an impact around the world, you could literally sell at the price of your choice.

This is the main idea of "selling on purpose." Don't tell people what you do or how you do it. Give the cause for why you do it because ultimately they are buying the story.

Having a profitable business by being the cheapest product on the market is becoming more difficult these days because of competition. If anything, I would advise going the other direction. I think that low-supply products could come to market and leverage their purpose to sell higher-priced goods centered around the idea that people are buying the story. Just as Picasso figured out years ago, they're not buying the painting, they're buying the story.

4.3 Persuasion in Slow Motion

> The more emotionally invested you are in something, the less objectively critical you become. This is the fundamental reason why marketing your purpose works.

At gas stations, there are ads on screens while you're pumping gas because even if it only takes thirty seconds, you are a captive audience for those thirty seconds. This might seem overstimulating, but the genius part about it is that it's giving us exactly what we want. People innately desire connection.

I'll watch people as they're waiting for the elevator. If they have to wait for the elevator at all, even just a few seconds, they pull out their phones. They'll look at something while they wait for those couple of seconds. Then they'll get in the elevator, and they'll be right back on their phone again for the seconds-long journey. We *want* to fill in the blank time with consumption. And each time one of those time lapses is filled, we are being influenced toward *something*.

We are constantly being influenced, and influence is just persuasion in slow motion. We're being influenced every day, not just in advertising but in the content we consume. If you take a step back, influence is hidden in plain sight. And it's everywhere. You can't escape it.

A prime example of this is alcohol. Today, it's pretty much accepted that any adult social event *should* have alcohol. It's easy to forget that, not that long ago, alcohol was so unaccepted in the United States that it was illegal from 1920 until 1933.

Prohibition was eventually repealed not because of a change in mindset but because of the rising rates of violent crimes associated with the illegal buying, selling, and transportation of alcohol. Enforcing the law was just impractical.

Coming out of Prohibition, alcohol was still not socially accepted. But a couple of decades later, we started allowing alcohol in ads on television. It didn't take long for this to radically shift the social perspective on alcohol in the United States. If you flood the market with enough images of people celebrating with toasts or relaxing on the couch with drinks, it becomes reality. It's easy to forget that this isn't how it's always been. **This is an engineered mindset.** Now, rather than associating beer with debauchery or immorality, we associate it with football on Sundays and majestic Clydesdales in the snow—or delivering cans of water for disaster relief efforts.... Influence prevails yet again.

Engineered Mindsets

An even better example of an engineered mindset is what happened with the diamond and the concept of engagement.

Prior to the modern era, there was no such thing as a wedding engagement. If you were a man in the 1930s, you went to the father of the woman you loved, and you **proposed** the idea of asking his daughter to marry you. Sometimes the woman's whole family was involved in the process. After you proposed this idea to her family, you would officially propose the idea to the woman. If she accepted, marriage came just a couple of months after that. Then De Beers® changed everything by pulling off one of the most successful advertising campaigns in the world.

De Beers® was founded in 1888 on the heels of a major diamond rush in South Africa. By 1938, De Beers® realized they were only selling these precious stones to very wealthy people. Princes, kings—only the upper echelon of society bought diamonds. They started toying with the idea of expanding their sales beyond this tiny percentage of the overall population. But how the hell are you going to sell shiny stones to commoners who have no use for them?

The solution was to paint the diamond as the ultimate symbol of eternal love—a tangible representation of a husband's everlasting commitment. De Beers® paid lecturers to go into high school auditoriums and explain to young women how real men signified their commitment with this thing called an engagement ring, which told everyone that this young lady was spoken for. She was off the market.

Of course, a diamond was a serious financial investment. How could De Beers® convince poor and middle-class men to spend their hard-earned money on a precious stone? Again, De Beers® had an ingenious response. Rather than a flat rate, they proposed that an engagement ring should match the level of a young man's income, representing about two months worth of his wages (an average engagement ring today is $4,000. Back then, it was a lot less).

Over time, De Beers® managed to artificially engineer this cultural activity. As a cultural control, they influenced women by creating the expectation of judgment: "Oh, you got engaged? Well, let me see the ring. Wow! He must really love you." Meanwhile, men would try to outdo other men. After all, the more money you made, the bigger ring you could afford. And if you decided to go above and beyond, it made a real statement. As inflammatory as it may sound, even in the papers, the ads blatantly suggested that the bigger the diamond, the more you loved your gal.

That's not to say there weren't problems in the beginning. They had an issue in the early 40s with adaptation in a few regions of the United States. The major feedback they were getting from perception polls was that people thought of an engagement ring like a wedding dress. You wore it once as a symbol, then took it off and put it away, which made it very difficult to justify making such a major financial commitment for such a tiny thing. In response, in 1948, they introduced the slogan, "A Diamond is Forever."®

Those four words summed it up perfectly. If your love is forever, then your engagement ring should be too. This is a symbol of love to wear all your life. You're going to have this from the day you get married until the day you die, and you'll pass it on to your grandchildren and great-grandchildren, who will see the love you had. A diamond is forever. It's part of your estate. And it doesn't lose its value, so you can sell it if you're ever in a pinch.

To help cement this idea, De Beers® began to give diamonds to film stars. Suddenly, diamonds were appearing all throughout Hollywood. Everyone on the silver screen had one. Every time a movie ran in a local theater, it was like one long advertisement for De Beers®, played to an impressionable, captive audience of a hundred or more people in the theater.

I doubt anyone at De Beers® ever imagined that when they invented the concept of a marriage engagement in 1938 to sell diamonds, it would become a worldwide societal norm that's still going strong over 80 years later. They sold the entire planet on the idea that love was synonymous with diamonds. But here's the really amazing part:

A diamond isn't even *worth* two months of a man's wages!

In reality, diamonds are not by any means rare. The process of excavation is a little pricey, but there are diamond clusters all over the world. In South Africa, there are millions upon millions of them. So instead of mining these diamonds and then shipping them off to a supplier, they instead put them in "diamond closets" to keep them off the market and create artificial scarcity. They intentionally keep the supply low, and since people are always getting engaged, there is always high demand. It's almost devious!

The story associated with the engagement ring creates perceived value—artificial value, in fact. Today, it would be considered highly unethical to have paid lecturers enter public schools to push a product like that. It wouldn't be allowed now, but back then, they exploited it. They figured out what worked, and they did the impossible: They found a way to sell shiny stones to *everyone*, all the way down to the poorest working-class Joes. How? By selling a story.

The Identity of Purpose

In the Western world, it's kind of interesting what happens when you ask someone who they are. Almost everyone leads with their occupation. "I'm Tim. I'm a video director." If someone asks you some more questions, you'll probably branch out into some of the roles you play. "I'm a father and husband. I have two kids. I like to play football and hockey." By the end of your description of yourself, you've really only described the temporal roles you play in your identity. This is precisely the mistake that brands make.

The problem with temporal roles is that they can change. What if my business goes under and my wife leaves me and takes the kids, and I break my leg so I can't play sports anymore? Is Tim still Tim? I'm no longer any of the things I described to you. Those roles were important to me, but they were not my identity. My identity exists at a much deeper level.

Identity is attached to the driving desires that sustain a person throughout their entire lifetime.

Until your brand can describe who it is—its driving purpose, its meaning for existence, its reason for being born—your target consumer doesn't know the brand's true identity. They simply see the brand as the identity of the temporal roles. Your company could change the services or products it offers at any time, depending on how you're going to adapt to the marketplace, but who the brand truly is should never waver.

Chapter 5:

An Epic Quest: The Structure of the Purpose-Told Story

While anyone can make a purpose statement, it's far more difficult to create a purpose story because it requires a deep understanding of story structure, event design and emotional payoff. Too many corporations just hang empty purpose statements on the wall as a forgotten mantra when they could have dynamic purpose stories that are perpetuated through their culture.

People don't relate with statements. They're just words. People relate with stories because they are reflections of the world in which they live.

Stories have a serious impact on the success of our lives, whether it's winning a job, getting a date, or justifying our life choices. Stories give evidence to the patterns of life, and it's all about context.

When we tell a story, we are essentially providing context to content. For instance, if I were to hold up two fingers and say nothing, this gesture may have no inherent meaning to you. However, based on your experience and the context in which you see the world, you might derive several possible meanings from it. Someone might think it's signaling the number two. Someone else might see it as representative of the letter *V*. Or maybe they'll think it's communicating the concept of "peace" or saying "goodbye." Until I tell the story of why I'm doing what I'm doing, you have no context for the content.

It's like the old saying "a spoonful of story helps the data go down." Until we understand the context of data, we cannot know its meaning. That's what stories do. They give meaning.

From chat-room gossip and bar room bragging to twenty-four-hour broadcast news and fictional dramas, comedies, and thrillers—you name it—there are stories all around us every day. And why is that? Because stories give us a better understanding of our world. Without stories, we would have to understand the world purely through personal experience. So today, in an environment where there is so much noise in the marketplace, it's essential that brands tell their authentic story to give context as to why they do what they do.

There are so many stories available to us today that we can't possibly tune in to them all. Our only choice is to pay attention to the good ones and bypass the rest. So how do you make your story more effective and more approachable for the audience?

An even more important question: Why is it that *some stories stick*, and others don't? Why do some stories compel us? Why is it that while some stories leave us sleepy, while others inspire us? The reason is, not all stories are created equal. Finding your brand's story will be the biggest asset to your company moving forward.

5.1 The Elements of Story

Remember back in Chapter One when I described our ancient ancestors telling stories around campfires beneath the stars? Oral storytelling is our primary method of conveying information, and our brains are engineered to deduce meaning in the form of story because stories follow the event structure of everyday life. In fact, when you share data, most people's minds automatically begin to decode the information into story form through associations from memory. Pattern recognition allows us to track the ups and downs of a line graph representing something like the S&P 500. But our inclination for context is what makes us wonder, "What's the story behind this massive decrease?"

Great teachers provide relevant examples to help their students retain information, but a great storyteller takes the audience on a journey and leaves that information in their hearts. The audience retains the data and are inspired to learn more. So instead of giving raw data, it is better to contextualize the data in story form from the start.

Most short brand stories follow the tried-and-true three-act structure:

- **Exposition**
- **Conflict**
- **Resolution**

At the final point of resolution, there is an insight where everything from before now makes sense. This is how you build suspense and interest. By integrating the above-mentioned elements into a three-act story structure, you can create the ultimate brand purpose story.

In the following pages, we'll take a look at how this can be done, as well as some of the key variations on this style. Without these three ingredients, no story is interesting.

> There's a very particular science to storytelling. Much like chemistry, if given the right ingredients and the right recipe, you can provoke emotion.

Key Ingredient #1: Interesting Characters

You must have strong characters who resemble personality archetypes. (These archetypes might be a Type A, Type B, extroverted, introverted, etc. Whatever they are, they should resemble real people in real life.)

You want the viewer to begin to predict what these characters will do. Since we relate to these characters in real life and know people like them, we kind of understand how they'll react in certain situations.

Key Ingredient #2: Uncertain Outcomes

Uncertain outcomes *hook* and *hold* the viewers' attention by violating the audiences expectations, you have them curiously guessing what will come next. You can generally always hold your audience via some level of conflict—something that needs to be resolved. In epic storytelling, it could be a magic ring that must be destroyed. In advertising, it might be the problem that your hero consumer will come in and solve at the end. Whatever it may be, the outcome must be unpredictable in order to be entertaining.

Key Ingredient #3: High Stakes (Jeopardy)

Every good story has something at stake. Whether it's life or death, winning or losing, getting the promotion or getting fired. Jeopardy makes the conflict interesting because, as the audience, we realize what can be won or lost. Ideally, the viewer feels empathetic toward the character and feels like the jeopardy is real. Having stakes to your story takes it from just reporting what happened to feeling that what's happening really matters.

High stakes for a purpose story could be the thing that will be lost if the brand doesn't help the world. Whether it's climate change, or global poverty, or a kid who can't afford to eat, showing what is at stake makes your cause a more worthy pursuit.

The Emotional Induction Experiment

In 2017, I met a man named Dr. Marvin Andujar at a tech convention in Tampa. He was a Computer Science Engineer professor with a fascination for neuropsychology. At the time, he was working in the field of brain-powered robotics and had created a league for brain-powered drone racing. I found it very novel that he could use a person's brain to control the complex flying movements of the drone, but even more so that he figured out an interesting relationship between the mind and machines.

After about a year of talking through ideas of how videos can affect people emotionally, I partnered with Dr. Marvin Andujar on an independent research project called the Emotional Induction Study. The goal of our research was to discover what specific variables in videos were responsible for inspiring audiences. We felt that by singling out the primary stimulus for emotion, we could amplify it and inspire audiences to a greater effect.

Most of us, at some time in our lives, have felt a strong emotional reaction to a video. For me, I can watch a short commercial, and in thirty seconds, I'm tearing up over a family-centered Publix® Thanksgiving ad. Or I get the goosebumps after watching a P&G® commercial about the Paralympics. But what was it specifically that caused these emotions? That is what this study sought to discover. Was it the captivating storyline, or the building music, or the cinematic shots? Was it the unique lesson learned or was it simply because the characters made you think about yourself and your own life?

After years of trying to discover this on my own, I came away with conflicting answers. The storytellers of the world like Robert McKee would say that emotional payout comes from the story—the amplitude between the positive and negative charges resulting in an emotional payoff. The cinematographers would swear that it is the moving visuals that take us to another world and make us feel things we've never felt. Neuroscientists would point to research that suggests that scenes merely provoke emotionally charged memories that are already in our minds, meaning the video is just the door to our own thoughts and not the actual motivator for emotion. Audio engineers would tell us that music unlocks our emotions, and that a well-played song can bring even a stone heart to tears.

My theory was that the emotional payoff from video is a delicate pattern of all of these factors—the exact same recipe repeated over and over, just cooked at different temperatures. As we conducted our first pilot study at the end of the year, we found some rather interesting results.

The Cognitive Psychology of Inspiration

During the pilot experiment, we took six participants from all different backgrounds and had them wear a number of biosensors while watching inspirational videos. Each participant would wear an EEG computer-brain interface device called a G-tec Sahara, which reads several regions of the brain to record alpha, beta, and theta waves. This data would then be shown in real time in response to the video to locate areas where brain activity spiked. After the brain activity was recorded, we would then use an algorithm to map the brain activity on an emotional spectrum compass to see what type of emotion was being felt at a particular time marker in the video.

In conjunction with the EEG device, we used a thermal recorder to detect rises in body temperature and a galvanic skin response sensor to measure sweat gland activity during emotional reactions. Similar to how your hands sweat on a first date, electrodermal activity represents micro-changes in sweat content throughout the body that change the electrical characteristics of the skin. This can be used to indicate how significant an emotion is and how long it was sustained. In addition to that, we had each participant wear a pulse oximeter to record any decrease or rise in pulse and blood oxygen levels, which would indicate that the heart was activated through the emotional arousal.

The videos we showed ranged from a heartwarming, snowy Christmas commercial from Apple®, to a heart-wrenching human rights advertisement for Right to Play, to an empowering journey of a young girl's life from Volvo®. We even tested one of our own videos that we created, which was a social experiment to spread awareness about PTSD.

Halfway through the day, one of our participants, a young hispanic female, started to have a very strong reaction to the PTSD video. She burst into tears, and so Dr. Andujar and I came into the observation room to interview her on the spot. After we calmed her down, we asked what was it that made her have such a strong reaction. She explained that three years prior, her best friend had committed suicide. For almost a year after this traumatic event, certain things were triggers for her. She would have to walk out of class or leave a restaurant to collect herself and calm her emotions. She went on to explain that when she saw that the characters in the video were experiencing what she had experienced, it took her back to that feeling. When asked exactly what she felt in her body, she described in detail an autonomous sensory meridian response (ASMR) that started from her upper neck and extended down her extremities to her fingertips.

It was very clear that the video connected to a strong memory that was still emotionally charged. When we asked her to describe what the emotion was that she was feeling, I found it odd that she used the word "comforting." She appeared to be anything but comfortable, but as Dr. Andujar and I returned to the control room, he began to plot her brainwave data on the emotional spectrum. All her activity was in the northeast region of this chart, characterized by positive valence, positive arousal, the area where empowerment, enjoyment, interest, and inspiration all lived.

Although this young woman appeared to be shaken up, the data and her own words both proved otherwise. It seemed that by watching a group of people who understood her reality and how she felt, the video struck a great sense of truth and belonging, even in the midst of a seemingly negatively charged memory.

At that moment, I wondered if that sense of belonging should be another variable we should look at as a contributor. Her brain activity after this video never did return to its original level, so we ended her session early and moved on to the next participant.

As the videos continued to play one by one, we watched the data in real time as the viewers' emotions spiked in sync at the climax of each of the videos. But one participant seemed to be an outlier. He was a seemingly normal caucasian middle-aged male. He was a father of two, and in his pre-interview, he mentioned that he enjoyed great stories. However, for one reason or another, the videos we chose just didn't provoke any emotion. Even the human rights ad and the PTSD experiment, which had gotten everyone else stirred up, evoked only a blip of emotion on his recordings.

On the last video, we decided to make a change. During the course of putting on all the biosensors for the experiment, this somewhat emotionless man talked rather passionately about coaching hockey and his love for the sport. It was a detail that had been seemingly irrelevant at the time. Before playing the final video, we did a quick search for inspirational hockey videos and came across a hometown Rangers® ad that showed how hockey brought communities together. We loaded up the file and pressed play.

Not even five seconds into the video, we saw his emotions begin to rise. His pulse increased, his temperature rose, and by the midpoint of the video, his emotional response was almost triple what it had been during all the other videos. As we finished up the pilot experiment that day and prepared to take all the data back to the lab, I couldn't help but wonder how this man, who had flatlined during the best inspirational videos we could find, lit up like a Christmas tree for the hockey ad.

I left that day even more curious than I had arrived. I had come looking for a specific element in videos that triggered emotional responses, and I left thinking, "Maybe it's not in the video. Maybe it's in the person."

We've known for years that really effective stories work best when the audience has a deep interest in the topic of the story, but this idea of what I called **inspirational iterest segmentation** was an eye-opening discovery in the study. In the broadcast age, marketers would put relevant commercials on the networks their target audiences were likely to watch. Hockey ads would likely be shown on sports networks that sports fans would watch, and diaper ads would likely be shown on networks like Lifetime® or Oxygen® that mothers would likely watch.

This isn't a new concept, but what's interesting to me is that now, because of big data, we have the opportunity to inspire micro-interest segments. We can take a deep understanding of the audiences' passions and make stories that specifically fit their unique worldview on a micro level. I began to wonder. Maybe we could even tailor-make stories that would guarantee a sense of belonging in these micro-interest groups. It was clear that my research was taking a turn and was far from done.

An Opportunity of a Lifetime

For weeks, I couldn't stop thinking about the man and the hockey ad. Why was I so interested in inspiring him?

I was intruiged by the challenge and, more importantly, the opportunity. We had so easily induced emotion in the other subjects, specifically the emotion of empowerment. In their interviews, they even used the words "inspiring," "empowering," and "uplifting" to describe their experiences with the videos. But this man was different. He was stone cold for four of the most emotional videos we could find, but came to life for a story relating to his passion.

Not long after the experiment, we had the CEO of one of the largest hospitals in Tampa come over to the office for a meeting. Over the course of our discussion, I begin to talk about the pilot experiment and some of our findings. Instantly, I could see a lightbulb go on in his head.

He proceeded to explain a problem shared by hospitals around the world. When a patient is admitted for treatment of an illness, disease, or injury, they spend the majority of their time lying in a bed, down on their health—and their luck. That physical state of lying in a confined room, listening to the beeping of medical equipment, can be the most uninspiring environment one can be in. However, research has proven that patients who maintain an optimistic outlook of their recovery and feel empowered to overcome their illness have faster rates of recovery and even statistically higher chances of survival. What's even more interesting is that in almost every modern hospital in America today, there are TVs perfectly positioned in patients' rooms that could deliver a message of hope to them.

I thought to myself, "Wow this is big!"

What if video could positively effect people's health? By creating stories that tapped into people's passions and empowered them to believe that they could overcome their circumstances, could we influence their optimism and ultimately influence their health outcome?

We parted ways and agreed to get back together in the coming year as our research progressed. I began to share this idea with other people, only to get crazy looks and blank stares in response, but I felt like there was something there. Just like the man and the hockey ad, it wouldn't be easy, but I needed to figure out how to systematically inspire different personas. I went back to the books, this time with deeper curiosity and direction.

Learned Expectations and Purpose Story Examples

Thanks to decades of American filmmaking and its established conventions, we have come to expect certain touchstones in our storytelling. These are the sorts of things you probably never even notice, yet when they are abandoned, something just feels *off*.

For example, we subconsciously expect the hero to come from the left of the frame. This originated in Western films, when the hero always came from the left so we could see his gun on his right hip. This established their power in the scene. Even today, we still see this happening. The president of the United States will almost always be captured on the left of the frame when shaking someone's hand, so he literally has the upper hand in the photo. Regardless of whether you consciously recognize these events when they are happening, your mind has built up an expectation that the good guy or hero is typically on the left.

Another timeless trick that comedians and storytellers alike use to entertain their audience is **the plot twist**. All good stories have a twist. In fact, good stories are like a good joke; the ending is always inevitable, yet surprising.

The twist is essential for good storytelling. We expect it. In films, the hero is betrayed by an ally closest to him during the final act. Or an expected complication turns everything on its head, and circumstances become worse than ever. Or, in the case of an anecdote, the stranger to whom you just spent five minutes venting about your jerk of a boss turns out to be your boss's best friend. Your audience is expecting you to end a story (or a joke) by revealing something they didn't know. This gives them a final rush of insight that allows them to apply greater meaning to the whole story.

Learned expectations like these are critically important when creating your purpose story because, regardless of how great the story is, it needs to follow the form that audiences are accustomed to. Otherwise, you may confuse them or let them down with a soft payoff.

As an audience is watching a video, a portion of the brain is capturing the information and applying meaning while another portion of the brain is trying to predict what will happen next. This predictive process is one of the most important areas we must focus on as storytellers. Imagine if someone was telling you a long-winded joke, and you predicted the ending within the first few seconds. At the end, the emotional payoff is low, and you may even feel like they've wasted your time.

The same thing is true with your purpose story. Depending on the audience and the setting, you should have a fifteen-second version, a one-minute version, and a long-form version, each of which has a dynamic twist of great meaning for the audience to realize. Here is an example of a fifteen-second purpose story involving John F. Kennedy and a janitor.

> *In 1961, John F. Kennedy was visiting NASA headquarters for the first time. During the tour, he saw a janitor who was cleaning the hall beside him. The president walked over to introduce himself and asked the janitor what his role was at NASA. The janitor replied, "I'm helping put a man on the moon."*

This story is short, simple, and to the point. It has a good twist in the end and moves quickly enough to keep your interest the entire time. John F. Kennedy would later use this story in one of his great American speeches to explain to the world that no matter who we are or what we do, we have a greater role to play as Americans. Instead of just telling the audience, "You have a greater purpose," which would have had little effect, by contextualizing that same message in a story that had a good twist, the audience received a rush of insight at the end, making the message more memorable. Now, let's take a look at a one-minute purpose story from one of my friends, Josh Pearson, who is a muralist in Tampa.

> *Twelve years ago, a man by the name of Jason Sowell created a nonprofit called "The Laundry Project."® The purpose of his nonprofit was to help people in the community that couldn't afford to clean their clothes*

by hosting a day at the laundromat where anyone could wash their clothes for free. After years of helping people all over the US, he decided he was going to add to his mission by leaving a colorful mural that said "Clean" on all the laundromats he went to. He hired a muralist, and they went to work.

The muralist began his first "clean" mural. He delicately filled in the letters from left to right, and as he finished up the final letter, a man came walking over from across the street. As he got closer, the muralist could see that he was crying. He asked the man "Are you okay?" and the man responded, "Thank you." Wiping away his tears, the muralist listened intently. He explained, "For fifteen years, I've been addicted to drugs and alcohol, and two months ago I finally got clean." The muralist set down his brush and listened closer. "Two weeks ago, I moved into the house across the street, and when I opened the door this morning and saw the message you wrote for me, I had to come over and say thank you. This will be my reminder every day to stay clean." The muralist stood there in shock as he looked back and could now see what it meant to be "clean."

This story unfolds the greater purpose of the muralist, the laundry project, and the man, all in one short twist at the end. Notice how each of these stories start by painting the setting and the main character.

Each story mentions what year it is, where we are, and what is unfolding in the scene. This is important because, as we discussed earlier, there is a learned expectation for what the audience should know right away. Also, your setting and character introduction create the expectation for what is to come. Notice how in the clean story, the word "clean" is used multiple times in association with clothes to reinforce its meaning. Then, after the twist, it is used in a completely different context in association with drugs. By putting emphasis on the initial story of laundry and charity, this makes the audience believe that these will be the important elements that pay off in the end.

This allows you to walk the audience in the opposite direction and defy their expectations when the seemingly meaningless part of the story becomes the most meaningful. By intentionally walking the audience in the opposite direction in the beginning, it allows for a greater rush of insight and emotional payoff in the end. This is a must in your purpose story as well. If your story is predictable, it will not be as effective. Consider how you can walk your audience in a different direction at first to make your twist more meaningful, and above all, don't just tell them your purpose; paint that picture in their head and let them discover it.

5.2 Story Archetypes

Many marketers believe that because they've been exposed to stories over the years, they're good storytellers. But that's like listening to the radio your whole life and believing you can compose a symphony. It takes a lot of practice in order to get the recipe just right, and even if you've got all the correct ingredients, it takes the precise combination of these ingredients to cook a story that's compelling or interesting or memorable.

In the following pages, I have outlined a few of the most popular story archetypes, but the most important thing to remember is that *a story, in its simplest form, is always about change.*

> **Without change, you don't have a story. You have an event.**

Events are boring. An event is simply data. A story always has transformation, and so must your purpose story. Often times, the greater the transformation, the greater the emotional payoff. When you're creating your purpose story, one effective technique is to study what stories resonate with you. You might be surprised to realize that these stories have simple-to-follow archetypal frameworks. I call this the art of **"story laundering,"** and it's been utilized by some of the greatest stories ever told.

The Founder's Passion Story

The **"Founder's Passion" story** is built on the idea that, prior to the inception of the company, there was something so profound that the founder wanted to go out and fix in this broken world that he or she built an entire business just to do it. Fixing this problem was the founder's personal passion and the purpose behind the brand.

In the founder's passion model, we present an image of the broken world through the lens of the founder's eyes so we can empathize with their passion. We show the founder toiling over whether or not to take action, whether or not to take the risk, whether or not to make the sacrifice to do what he or she feels is right.

In 2017, Budweiser® used this story archetype with an "immigrant story" commercial that aired during the Super Bowl®. The commercial showed the founders coming over to America from Europe, preparing to start a whole new life. The commercial presented the idea that these immigrants had a passion to make the all-American beer, one that would be a symbol of opportunity and the embodiment of the American dream. Through hard work and dedication, they built this small craft beer company and grew it into the giant Anheuser-Busch® corporation that we know today. This is a story of an underdog prevailing against the forces of uncertainty and antagonism by leaving the comfort of his home to start a new life with a greater purpose.

This is a timeless structure for brand stories because many great companies that exist today were once just an idea inside the mind of a restless entrepreneur—a little spark that kindled countless moments of action. This story is almost identical to the Hero's Story archetype, which we'll review shortly, but the key factor with this archetype is that the founder's passion is the protagonist and the main point of emphasis. That is the focus and the driving force. It is the main thing that changes throughout the story from a dream to reality. This is the source of the amplitude of the story, from a little spark in a child's mind to a burning passion fueled by the determination for the founder to fulfill it.

The Mirror Story

At the highest level of brand storytelling is something called the **"Mirror" story**. Achieving a successful mirror story is when your audience goes from just watching the character in your story to *becoming* the character in your story. They place themselves in the character's shoes and begin to predict what they would do in that situation. They begin to see what's happening in the video as a parallel of their own lives, thereby creating a dynamic in which your audience feels as if they're a part of your story. They feel the stakes of your character and are empathetic to the wins and losses of the character.

Then comes the twist!

Just when the audience is feeling most connected with the character, you violate the expectation of the viewer. Something happens that flies in the face of the obvious outcome, creating suspense. The viewer is now entangled in what the outcome of the story may be. These are the commercials that glue people to the screen. Even if they don't particularly care about the product, they want to know how this mini-story is going to end.

In a purpose-driven mirror story, you start by painting a picture that is identical to the worldview and perspective of the consumer. For the Budweiser® example above, it may go something like this. "I was working nine to five every day, going to work and running the rat race, until I asked myself, 'Am I really contributing to the world or just helping people buy more stuff?' So I decided to pack my bags and pursue a life where I could do something greater."

Painting a picture that is general to the sort of emotions most people have, like being discontent at work, connects the audience more closely to you and your story. Chances are, most people who hear your purpose story won't be big-shot business owners who weathered the entrepreneurial journey, so this story archetype is built around relatedness, risk, twist, and pursuit.

The most important part is to establish the risk and take it. That character's courage to do what is difficult is what the audience is rooting for. So, in this story archetype, it's best to be vulnerable in the character introduction so you can show the transformation of overcoming those faults by taking the risk and pursuing the purpose.

The Hero's Journey

One of the most popular brand storytelling archetypes is the **"Hero's Journey."**

Joseph Campbell's book *A Hero with a Thousand Faces* presented the theory that there was one singular "monomyth" in ancient Greek mythology that could be found repeated in the myths and creation stories of human cultures around the world. Campbell claimed that although all these myths appeared wildly different, *the structure of the stories was nearly identical at the most basic level.* In fact, once you learn to see it for what it is, you'll quickly realize that the hero's journey is everywhere. Books, commercials, and films use it all the time. Movies like *Star Wars*® and *The Matrix*® follow the hero's journey nearly to the letter—even *Happy Gilmore*®.

The hero's journey starts with an underdog. The underdog comes into a broken world. They meet a mentor who gives them a gift and presents the hero with a call to adventure. Over the course of the adventure, the hero experiences a moment of triumph and brings about a restored world.

In the Biblical story of Exodus, Moses (the hero) starts as the underdog and enters the broken world of Egypt, where his people are enslaved. God (the mentor) speaks to Moses in the form of a burning bush and tells him to return to Egypt and free his people (call to adventure). Moses parts the Red Sea by using his staff (the gift), which lets his people flee while the enemy is swallowed by the sea (moment of triumph), leading his people to the promised land (restored world).

In *The Matrix*®, Neo (the hero) is an underdog who finds Morpheus (the mentor) in a dream. Morpheus gives Neo the option of a blue pill or a red pill (call to adventure). He takes the gift of knowledge and training from the mentor, goes into a broken world, becomes a hero, and saves it.

In *Star Wars*®, the underdog is Luke Skywalker (the hero) who meets Obi-Wan Kenobi (the mentor) who teaches him how to use the gift of the force (the gift) and tells him he needs his help saving a captured princess (call to adventure).

Luke blows up the Death Star (moment of triumph) and saves the galaxy (restored world).

Examples of the hero's journey abound. The point is, in the same way that the hero's journey archetype works in entertainment, mythology, and religious stories, it also works perfectly for the Purpose Story—*if* you understand your role.

I've found that the pervading mistake in the hero's journey story is that most brands make the unconscious mistake of positioning themselves as the hero. While that may seem logical from a marketing standpoint, this can be perceived as a vanity tactic. What you should do is *make your consumer the hero of the story.*

Position the consumer as the hero of the story—the underdog who gets the gift from the mentor, answers the call to adventure, and saves the world. You, the brand, are the mentor.

This is actually easier than it sounds. The consumer is already the underdog because everyone in their own life feels like they are the underdog. They can empathize. As the mentor, you're giving them your product, which is the magical gift to save the world. You're showing them the way to become the hero in their own story.

Tesla® is a great example of this. On the surface, Tesla® is a car company, but their mission statement is "to accelerate the world's transition to sustainable energy." Notice that their mission is to help accelerate *the world* to more sustainable energy. They're not the ones doing it. They're empowering others to be the heroes. They're just helping; they're the mentor showing the way, holding the flashlight to the promised land, and we can only assume that if everyone accepts their ideology, they can become the hero. (I'll talk about this in more detail in Chapter 6.)

If you find that you've subconsciously positioned your company as the hero of your own story, that's natural. In fact, in some forms of your purpose story it may make more sense. But if you can restructure your brand's story and reposition yourself as the mentor who's helping the hero—the consumer, the world, or whomever—you will come off as a much more meaningful brand.

5.3 The Purpose-Driven Formula

In Chapter One, we talked about the old tactics of inadequacy marketing. The three-step approach of inadequacy marketing was to:

1. Find the hurt
2. Amplify the pain
3. Heal the wound

Cue the black and white video of poor, old mom pushing around a vacuum cleaner. It's getting stuck. It's heavy. It's slow. She's missing out on time with her kids. Then the voiceover comes in and says, "There's got to be a better way!" Then, *bang!* The screen transitions to full color, and the woman is dancing around the kitchen with a Swiffer. This advertising formula has been so overplayed that it has reached the point of meta-comedy.

Back in its heyday, the inadequacy marketing model was the preferred method of interruptive advertising because you only had about thirty seconds to pitch that sucker. But, as we've seen, the problem is that today's evolved audience can spot this sort of manipulation within seconds. For trendy consumers, if an ad starts out by prodding at pain points, they know exactly what's to come. Today, the only way to capture their attention is through the polar opposite of inadequacy marketing: inspirational and empowerment marketing.

Storytelling and Empowerment Marketing

In empowerment marketing, the key ingredients are below.

1. Find the consumer's **passion**
2. Amplify their **potential**
3. Become their **partner**

In the end, as opposed to healing a wound, you play the role of the lifelong mentor. You present your hero with something that will aid in their journey. Your purpose aligns with their passion. The audience is now reacting not from the lack of something, but from the existence of value, purpose, morality, etc.

In this new model, companies are trying to create a deep connection through like-mindedness. Using shared values as a marketing attraction method at the top most part of the funnel is one way to ensure you are attracting the right consumers.

Apple® does a great job with this. Their ads really just show people doing what they love—creatives out taking pictures on their iPhones of mountain ranges, or on their laptops editing videos in alleyways—and they connect to their consumers' passion right away. Then they amplify their potential. The message is, this product lets you be even better at what you already love doing. Nike® does the same thing. Purposeful messaging for them is like saying, "Sports are awesome. We want you to be the best athlete you can be. We're here to help you reach your goals."

Being a partner to your consumer is acknowledging their prerogative to decide whether or not to do business with you.

This isn't a transactional relationship. It's not a call to action. You're not telling people to call this 800-number right now for free shipping and handling. You're saying, "We believe what you believe, and we're here to partner with you and help you grow." In the absence of that oh-so-famous call to action, the audience feels empowered that it's their decision.

Chapter 6:

Won on Passion

Traditional advertising seeks to move consumers through a sales funnel, moving from the widest category, Attention, down through Interest and Desire to Action. The popular **AIDA** model below shows the responsibility of the marketer to incrementally push consumers down the sales funnel to the point of purchase.

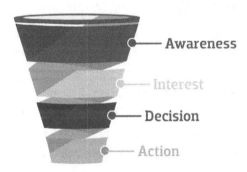

Figure 1.1

The problem with this model is that every funnel contains friction, and any doubt that creeps into the consumer's mind can push them right back out of the funnel before they get to the point of purchase. But what if there was a way to grease the funnel to ensure more conversions? Better yet, what if there was a way to make one-time consumers into lifetime consumers, perpetuating them through the funnel?

Well, there is. And it's easier than you think. The name of the game is **brand loyalty.**

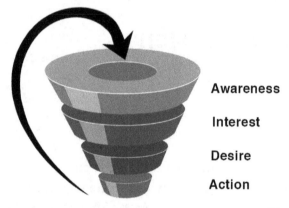

Awareness

Interest

Desire

Action

Figure 1.2

6.1 Brand Loyalty

Have you ever seen someone who's crazy in love? They may act strangely or even completely irrationally because they're so devoted to this person. They are emotionally blinded. The dream for brands is to elicit this sort of head-over-heels, irrational love from their consumer base. So, how can we achieve this? By creating higher-quality products? By selling at the lowest prices? By running a sale every other weekend?

Think again.

Over the years, successful salesmen have found that the secret to selling is connecting with your clients beyond the level of the sales transaction. Car salesmen have been known to do this by sending birthday cards to past consumers to keep the relationship going, and doctors have followed up with patients long after their appointment to ensure that they are doing well. This level of caring about the client will not only keep you in mind, but also helps breed brand loyalty.

The law of reciprocity says that if you give, you will receive. However, very few companies are **giving at scale** in the digital age.

> **Brand loyalty is when a consumer chooses your brand over the competition over and over again, even when your product is more expensive or inferior to a competitor.**

Building brand loyalty is one of the most effective sales strategies there is because the more loyal a consumer becomes toward a brand, the less objectively critical their decision-making is in buying your product. At the highest levels, brand loyalty breeds **brand ambassadors.** Brand ambassadors are consumers who not only buy your product over and over again but evangelize your brand to their friends and family. They become free marketing for your brand. And your brand essentially becomes part of their lifestyle. They perpetuate your horizontal marketing efforts.

We've seen this happen with brands like Apple® and Patagonia® who have created an almost cult-like following. Another brand who has been able to do this at scale is Harley Davidson®. Harley Davidson's® purpose is to help others fulfill their dream of personal freedom. They empower their consumers to "feel free," and they have created a community of brand ambassadors who ride nothing but Harley® motorcycles because they buy into that purpose.

Harley® is not just a motorcycle brand. They are the symbol of a lifestyle of adventure and connection. Since its inception in 1903, Harley® has become the most tattooed brand in the world. By empowering consumers through shared values—inspiring them to be your brand ambassadors and to multiply that mindset—you turn the sales funnel into a **sales vacuum** that feeds itself.

6.2 Where is Your Consumer Going?

In the early 2000s, Netflix®, a small DVD-rental-by-mail and video streaming company, tried to broker a deal to sell their company to Blockbuster® for $8 million. Blockbuster® didn't buy it. They were an $8 billion business at the time, and $8 million would have been a drop in the bucket. But they were doing just fine, and people were never going to stop renting movies in their stores, right?

Blockbuster® didn't have the vision to see that DVDs by mail and video streaming were the future of video. They didn't innovate. They didn't evolve. They just stuck with the status quo. They thought people were never going to stop renting videos. As a consequence of their inability to change, they went bankrupt in 2010, and Netflix® is now one of the biggest, most profitable companies on Earth.

What Blockbuster® should have done was to conduct a brand audit. They should have asked, "What's our strategic position in the market? Something we can give back that no one else can?" They were the biggest force when it came to brick-and-mortar stores, but they weren't able to see that brick-and-mortar stores were no longer the only way consumers shopped. Like Wayne Gretzky says, "Don't go to the puck, go to where the puck is going." Had Blockbuster® understood **where their consumer was going**, they would still be in business today.

Netflix® was passionate about removing all obstacles for the consumer. They gave the consumer greater convenience and knew how the consumer wanted to get their entertainment.

You can't help but wonder what entertainment would look like today if Blockbuster® had bought Netflix® when it had the chance. Blockbuster® could have taken over. Maybe we would all be binge-watching Blockbuster® on our phones. Instead, they shut their doors. So, where is your consumer going?

New Tech and ROI

The Blockbuster® catastrophe certainly wasn't the first time a major company has made a disastrous tech-based oversight in the digital era. When we first stepped foot into the Digital Age, we had massive volatility of disruption, especially with the internet. In those early days of Web 1.0, we simply weren't ready for what the internet was going to be. The potential wasn't entirely clear, and the vision faltered a bit.

For one thing, we initially overvalued the marketplace. Domain names were selling for up to $1 million dollars—just the domain name! It cost roughly $50,000 to hire a professional web development team to build a simple, clunky website that basically looked like a Word document with hyperlinks. Even for many major companies, the viability didn't make sense, especially if the purpose of your site was to sell a two-dollar product that people would have to go to a store to buy anyway. Where is the ROI on that?

These days, you can buy a domain for five dollars, build a website for ten bucks, and sell millions of dollars of inventory with little plug-ins. People working from home can have lucrative businesses because of this quick evolution of technology.

Marketing seems to be a laggard when it comes to evolution. Sure, there are new tools each year and digital is opening new doors, but we've been leveraging the same three main channels for sixty years now.

Audiences have an expectation for evolution. You see this across the board. Every year, you can expect a new iPhone® that is re-engineered to make my life better in some way. There are constantly new types of cars, gizmos, and gadgets. But what do consumers get from marketing? The same thing, year after year.

Whether it's the annoying pop-up I get when I'm trying to read an article online or an interruptive ad that takes me away from my favorite sports programming, audiences assume that these things are going to evolve. For the brands that don't evolve, that's when we really see the disconnect. Younger audiences do not have the patience to put up with the same old ads over and over again. The will eventually begin to abandon the media channel entirely, which is what we are seeing with cable-cutters.

The Next Generation: Gen Z

We've talked a lot about Millennials in this book, but let's not forget, there is a new cohort coming down the line: Generation Z. And if you think Millennials are demanding and have short attention spans, you haven't seen anything yet.

Gen Z is the first generation comprised of truly digital natives. They live in an instant world. They've grown up with the internet and don't know what life is like without it; they were literally born online.

In the days of the dial-up modem (remember that sound?) I sat there for five minutes, eagerly waiting to get online. Studies today show that Gen Zs will abandon a page if it fails to load in less than three seconds. The concept of connection was synonymous with "load time" back in the day, but now Gen Z assumes high-speed connectedness. And you can bet they will also expect evolution.

Millennials and Gen Zs are almost always partaking in **"dual-consumption of media."** That means using two connected devices at once, whether a phone and a computer or a TV and a phone. This has been noted during NFL® games. During commercial breaks, there is a major spike in social activity because Millennials and Gen Zs don't watch the commercials. They get on their phones. Some bloggers have affectionately nicknamed this population "crotch surfers" because they literally look down at their laps and engage in social media for three minutes until the program comes back on. *They are not even watching the commercials these companies pay so much to broadcast.* Why would they? They'd rather see their friends' lives than watch someone trying to sell them an overpriced fruit juicer. They lift their heads back up when the football game comes back on, and the spike in social media activity goes back down.

How Early is Too Early?

They say the early bird gets the worm, but as for the early worm … he gets eaten. While Blockbuster® shut down because of their inability or unwillingness to innovate, the opposite can also occur. If the market isn't ready, your brand might end up like the early worm instead of the early bird.

In 1993—long before the iPhone®, let alone the iPad®—Apple® released the Newton, a portable tablet computer. They brought it to market, thinking it was going to be huge. After all, it was the logical next step in the evolution of the personal computer. But the market wasn't ready. The Apple® Newton flopped.

Later, when smartphones were gaining popularity, Apple® saw the direction the marketplace was headed. Instead of taking another run at the PDA® product line, they used the same technology of the Newton® and inserted it into another new up-and-coming device: the smartphone. The iPhone® quickly became the highest-selling smartphone of all time.

The best way to explain this is to look at the way populations move. Every market has a *"leading edge" segment*. These are the early adopters. They are always innovating and trying new things. You don't see mass adoption until the rear portion of that leading edge begins to adopt. Then the general public sees what these innovators are using, and they adopt it. But if *no one* other than those innovators picks up on a new product, it's dead in the water.

I tried to be the first to market in early 2010. I thought 3D TVs were going to be the next big thing in home entertainment. I thought these things were going to be *huge*. My company started shooting on 3D cameras with dual optics before anyone else was doing it. Not only did you have to zoom and focus, but you had to use a conversion angle toggle to create the 3D effect, which pitched the two optics toward each other. It was very difficult to adapt this new technology, but we thought there would be a great demand in the marketplace— everyone was going to have 3D TVs! We had to adapt, right? Manufacturers were churning out 3D TVs. Blu-ray 3D movies started to be produced. Satellite providers like DIRECTV® started producing programs for 3D TVs. Everyone in the video market was convinced this was the direction entertainment was headed.

But then people looked at it and realized … this technology just isn't that great. Who wants to have special glasses on their face the whole time they're watching TV? You don't really get the feeling of 3D unless you move your head to get the parallax effect. And what about watching TV while you're doing things around the house? Are you going to wear these glasses all the time?

3D TV, as it turned out, was not the next big thing; it was a fad. But almost simultaneously, another new thing came out called the smart TV. A TV connected to the internet, able to download apps like a smartphone. Nowadays, every TV is a smart TV.

Just like Web 1.0, the problem is that the product (3D TVs) was introduced before the technology was ready. 3D TVs have faltered and slipped. The technology *will* come back, and when it does, it's going to be incredibly good. Sometimes, you have to put a product out to market multiple times. If it's too early, you may just have to wait. The same is true with your purpose story. Keep in mind you are on the leading edge, so don't expect acceptance immediately. It may take time.

The Mistake of Advertising on Social Media

I have an outstanding bet with my friend right now that in three years, Facebook® will no longer be the king of social.

I've based this on a study the European Union conducted called the Global Social Media Impact Study. When teens were asked about Facebook® in this study, they said their primary use for Facebook® was to stay in touch with older relatives. The teens proceeded to describe Facebook's® future as "dead and buried." More recent studies have shown that teenagers are flocking to Instagram® and Snapchat®, while Facebook® users are trending older. But I don't think this has as much to do with the older relatives or any sort of vague "cool" factor. I theorize it has everything to do with ads.

Facebook® spent years as a free-to-use, ad-free service. Other comparable services relied on saturating their sites with advertising (such as Friendster® and Myspace®), and people jumped ship. It's not that Facebook® was more selfless in this regard. They just had a better grasp of the game. They understood that eyes equaled dollars. They allowed their user base to grow ad-free for a long time, knowing all the while that more people in their playground now meant more money in their pockets later.

Now, Facebook®, like its predecessors, is saturated with ads. The news feed is filled with sponsored content. The second you see ads, it has a repulsive effect. We have seen the backlash against Facebook® for doing this, and they've even initiated some apology campaign attempts to try to re-earn user trust. My point is, *your brand can't just hope to stay relevant by marketing to the kids on social media.*

This oversaturation problem has happened in every form of media up until now, and we still haven't learned from it. In fact, Facebook® bought Instagram®, and what's Instagram® doing now? The same thing. It's starting to be saturated with ads and sponsored content. Eventually, it too will reach a critical mass where ads start having an adverse effect on the audience.

Is there a way to change this so marketing doesn't look like an ad, feel like an ad, or smell like an ad? How do we re-engineer this model to be effective? There is a way, and it's called **"branded entertainment"** (more on this in Chapter 9).

6.3 Clarity of Purpose

In the previous chapter, I talked about Tesla's® mission statement: "to accelerate the world's transition to sustainable energy." Again, their mission statement says nothing about being a car company. It says nothing about improving transportation. It's what they believe in. And this is not just an empty claim about what they do or what they stand for. They're actually out there doing it.

When hurricanes hit Puerto Rico, Tesla® was there. When the entire island went dark, their engineers set up a solar panel electrical grid to power the children's hospitals on the island. For them, it was more than just making sure that Puerto Rico was going to recover. It was a case study for the world stage. It proved that the power we are all relying on today is unstable and unreliable. Meanwhile, solar panels kept an entire island running just fine while traditional power was out for weeks.

Honda®, on the other hand, was one of the first major automakers to nail down hybrid technology. They filed for so many patents on the technology that it became difficult for anyone to compete with them. In fact, the reason you don't see as many hybrid cars on the market today is because Toyota® and Honda® own a majority of all the hybrid technology. Then Tesla® came out and basically said, "Not only are we going to build the best electric car, but we're going to open-source the technology. We're going to give you the blueprints for free." While it would have been much more profitable to lock down all the intellectual property, they kept it open source so that other manufacturers could aid in their greater mission to transition to sustainable energy. Now that is operating according to your purpose!

Tesla's® message to the marketplace is, we don't even care about being the personal champions of sustainable energy. Our greater purpose beyond the accumulation of market share is to advance the world to more sustainable energy, even if that means giving it away. This builds goodwill not only with their consumers but also with people who couldn't afford to be their consumers because they may benefit in the future from Tesla's® dedication to innovate. Meanwhile, they are making big business moves. When they opened preorders for the Tesla® Model 3, they received 400,000 preorders in two days valuing at $8 billion, which is an unprecedented number for the automotive industry.

Tesla's® actions were purpose-centered. Remember the example of the Dove® Inner Beauty campaign? The collective reaction from consumers was: Wow! A brand that really cares. Let me ask you this: If I were to ask your consumers if your brand cares, what would they say? Is there tangible proof that your brand truly cares? Do you make actionable decisions like Tesla® and Dove® that show your purpose is greater than profit?

Chapter 7:

The Moral Dilemma

In 1988, the pastor of a small church in Michigan named Dan Seaborn made sixty handmade bracelets for the youth in his congregation.

Dan had just finished reading a 1986 book by minister Charles Sheldon called *In His Steps*, subtitled *What Would Jesus Do?* The next day, he came up with the idea of making bracelets featuring the letters "WWJD?". What started out as sixty bracelets grew to more than 50 million bracelets just a year later, and his product would eventually spread across the world. Dan had created something of meaning. These bracelets provoked curiosity from the marketplace, causing anyone who saw them to instantly ask, "Hey, what does that mean?" It also started a conversation about something much more meaningful.

Those four letters began to accomplish the very purpose that the pastor had been trying to achieve. Not only were these bracelets a wearable reminder to help keep us accountable for our actions, but they represented a story to tell others. A little bracelet became the symbol of a message that was told over and over again. Today, nobody even knows the actual number of WWJD® bracelets sold over the years. Some say it is upwards of 200 million. And that doesn't include the other merchandise that emerged bearing the WWJD tagline. People started replicating these products all across the world, spreading the movement. (Dan didn't get any royalties on these products, but that wasn't his purpose. His purpose was to start the movement.)

I wouldn't call the WWJD movement a "campaign," per se, but it is definitely an example of meaningful purpose in action. And it's proof that you don't need millions of dollars or an ad agency to do it. With buy-in from just a few followers, a purpose story can achieve a viral effect. This is an amazing case study in peer-to-peer horizontal marketing without the assistance of the internet.

7.1 Brand Survival in the Backlash Era

Today, we live in a morally volatile marketplace. Many baby boomers grew up in a world where there was left and right, there was male and female, and there was right and wrong—a code of ethics that the majority agreed on. There was sort of an unspoken agreement across the nation that this was the world, and these were the rules.

And then the Millennials came, decided this was their generation, and turned everything upside down. They blurred the lines on everything we thought we knew.

The modern era has seen an upsurge in social justice and purpose-driven idealism in the mind of consumers. While we know people are more diverse than their political affiliations, the numbers tell us that there are basically two Americas: red and blue.

Blue America seems to fully embrace social justice and purpose-driven idealism. Red America hasn't turned the corner fully when it comes to social justice, but it believes in purpose-driven idealism. The more strongly a movement appeals to the ideals of one side, the more likely the other side is to reject it.

When purpose is the source of differentiation, it has the potential to turn from a short-term fad into a long-term trend. Millennials are more united when it comes to counterculture beliefs than any other generation before. The tricky part, of course, is that values are never universal. As such, it can actually become a liability for a brand to make strong value claims one way or another. They could potentially lose a good portion of their audience.

A clear understanding of your target audience becomes critical. Coming out in strong favor of sustainable energy will galvanize a certain segment of your consumers, but you cannot do this without alienating someone else. For instance, the blue-collar worker whose job is threatened by environmental reforms. So, whose opinion is most important to your brand?

For example, we've had a number of mass shootings throughout the years, and every time a mass shooting happens, the media explodes with calls for stronger gun control. The accessibility and visibility of social media increase the ferocity of the backlash, and anytime consumers really get behind these kinds of social movements, they put pressure on brands to change.

After the shooting at Marjory Stoneman Douglas High School in Parkland, Florida in 2018, it was brought to the attention of the media that a major airline was providing discounts to National Rifle Association® (NRA) members on flights to annual NRA meetings. This had been done for years, and it wasn't even something that many NRA members knew about. But in the minds of many consumers, the fact that this airline was doing this showed that they aligned themselves with the opposing force in the gun control issue. After all, by giving discounts with these people, wasn't that as good as saying they approved of the NRA's stance against gun control?

From an ideological standpoint, this seems like a pretty far stretch. Barely anyone was even taking advantage of the discounts. But the brand was at the mercy of the public. This airline service with many competitors was at risk of a major decline in sales for not aligning with the volatile values of its consumers. Their response was to stop giving discounts to NRA members. Cue the backlash from supporters of the NRA. Some conservative politicians even took it upon themselves to take action to revoke tax breaks on fuel for the airline. How was it that in just two weeks' time, a non-issue turned into a national issue? It's because public opinion is now heavily influencing the marketplace. This is some slippery ground brands are treading on. Nobody made a big deal about the NRA discounts in the several years prior, but once something bad happened, consumers were quick to find someone to blame. This is the reality that brands will have to learn to deal with.

Uber® is another fascinating brand to dissect. They have dealt with a lot of issues and allegations in recent years. To begin with, their main competition is a highly established industry that has been around for decades: taxi services. To hear some of the stories surrounding this issue, you'd almost think there was a taxi mafia out there.

One problem arose in 2017 when Uber® advertised that their drivers were earning a certain rate, when in fact, the rate was actually based on the market and varied from city to city. In the New York market, Uber® drivers believed they were getting paid unfairly. At the same time, a slew of sexual harassment allegations and accusations of treating women unfairly in the workplace all became public knowledge. This boiled up into a serious issue for the brand. The following week, a #DeleteUber movement was trending. It resulted in over 500,000 people total deleting the Uber® app.

What an incredible response from consumers! Could you imagine a half of a million consumers leaving your platform over a social issue? That could be life-threatening for many brands. This case is just one of many that have happened in recent years in which consumers have chosen which brands thrive. This new idea of "**corporate euthanasia**" is one we are all familiar with but nobody seems to talk about. We, the public, chose to lay Blockbuster® to rest in early 2010 because they no longer were needed. We pulled the plug on Toys "R" Us® in 2018 and forced them into bankruptcy. We cost Uber® millions of dollars by deleting their app from our phones. We, as consumers, did this because we voted against them with our dollars. When consumers organize their spending habits based on their values, it's called "**dollar voting,**" and today, consumers are voting with their dollars to determine which brands will live and die in the new world.

These are the sorts of issues companies have always had to deal with, but the age of allowing a story to "blow over" is dead and gone. Issues come out every day, eventually bubbling up to the surface and creating a vast impact on how brands are perceived in the public eye.

Within the twenty-four-hour media cycle, there are minute-to-minute negative implications for a company if it doesn't live up to the moral standards of the general public that can affect a company or an entire industry overnight. That is very scary because the public's moral standards are so volatile.

We see companies scrambling to respond to even the slightest whiff of a scandal for fear of public backlash. Brands are not averse to firing just about anybody on their roster, even forcing CEOs and founders to step down if it means mitigating the impact of bad press.

7.2 The Movement of Social Movements

I believe there are two social movements on the near horizon that seek to reduce the disparity in income between corporations and consumers, as well as overcome the injustice of false media and the oppression of corporate propaganda. Almost all major social movements are based on the fundamental principle of rebalancing inequalities among members of society. Whether it is race, gender, sexual orientation, income, opportunity, or freedom, social movements occur in order to level the playing field and attain justice and equality.

We've always had social movements. They are nothing new, but they have never been able to have the kind of voice they now have in the age of participation. Social media has allowed groups of people to amplify the reach of their beliefs. As a result, social change has never been as volatile or as effective as it is today.

As dollar voting continues to become more popular, I believe the ideals of conscious capitalism will be incentivized by consumers and will be necessary in order for many businesses to survive. However, for companies who are resistant to adopting social and environmental practices into their business model, I forecast that there will be a social movement that aims to expose irresponsible brands on a global scale. In the same way that #DeleteUber was a micro-movement aimed at resetting the scale of pay equality and workforce responsibility, I foresee a time when several major brands in our age die a quick death at the hands of upset consumers who expose their malpractices to the masses. As consumers, we are realizing that we have enough choices of TVs or cars to purchase; if a company is acting irresponsibly, we can boycott them with our dollars and send a message to the rest of the industry.

Over the next few years, as consumers come to understand their true power in the marketplace, they may unleash social movements of greater power and reach. Movements like #OccupyWallStreet showed us that if consumers ever find themselves at odds with corporations, they can be a relentless force that demands change. After all, consumers are the fuel that corporations need to survive, so when corporations act in a way that hurts the consumer, consumers can return the favor. Get ready for a major dollar voting movement on the horizon.

The second movement I see coming is a movement against false news. The problem right now is that the media is incentivized to produce news quickly—not accurately. You can see the issue with this. The first station to put up something that's breaking rarely gets the story right. Over time, we have seen major discrepancies between CNN®, FOX News®, MSNBC®, etc., and how they interpret stories. Who can you really believe? As Denzel Washington once said, "If you don't read the newspaper, you're uninformed. If you do read it, you're misinformed." I'm not sure which is worse.

In an information-rich, hyperconnected world, you have access to all the information, all the time. People are fact checking in real-time. News stations are fact-checking other new stations, so they essentially undermine their own intelligence. Not only are there attacks from critical consumers, but there are attacks from competitors, resulting in massive distrust.

My personal prediction is that this all has a saturation point of critical mass. I think as the news evolves, there will come a breaking point when someone says something that represents a totally misconstrued reality, resulting in a major impact on the world. Today, we make decisions on the perception of reality just as much as reality itself. Elon Musk tweeted that he was thinking about buying Tesla® back, and overnight, the stock price rose dramatically. Just the perception that he would buy it caused a real shift.

In 2017 in Hawaii, during a test of the emergency system, a state-wide text accidentally went out warning of a nuclear attack. In response to the text, there were several reported suicides, all just from the *perception* that an attack to a nuclear event was about to happen. These unfortunate circumstances show what is at stake when we play with perceptions. I foresee that someone in the news will eventually take it too far, and the response from the public will be the same as it is for any brand: "This is not okay. #Deletenews."

It seems like a logical progression from where we're at today.

Influence over Income

If you think about it, the power of passion is a hugely effective long-term strategy because telling a consistent, passionate story not only positions you as the brand that cares the most, but will do the most for the consumer.

For years, the focus has been on the wrong part of the sales funnel. A brand must reset its mindset from targeting people as profit. They really need people's ears, eyes, hearts, and minds. Then the dollars will come. Targeting profits diminishes the view of lifetime value. The real target is **influence**.

When it comes to purpose, passion, inspiration, etc., the most common question that established brands have is, if there's no ROI in this, why do it?

In the new economy, influence is the new currency.

Brands need to realign their focus in this regard. If your brand's only focus is on profitability, you'll soon find yourself tip-toeing across the public stage at the first sign of backlash from your consumers. Instead, start with winning the hearts and minds of your consumers. Ultimately, that will lead to long-term profitability. The whole *Sold on Purpose* model is about re-aligning your value proposition to include a win for the consumer's future so the consumer is buying both your product and their better future.

If you're not yet convinced, the next chapter offers a more in-depth look at how indirect messaging is the new direct messaging.

Chapter 8:

Humility is the New Vanity

With all this talk about operating according to purpose, it might be tempting to call a big press conference and announce your brand's commitment to an enormous, idealistic mission. But the purpose story doesn't have to be about saving lives or changing the world. Instead of some esoteric quote about being a mighty force for good. Answer the simple question, *how can you use your talents to empower people?* In fact, the old "savior of the world" approach is sometimes the surest way of shooting yourself in the foot.

Several years ago, during the "green" marketing movement, brands all over the world started jumping on the bandwagon to market their companies' eco-conscious efforts, attempting to position themselves as heroes of sustainability.

In this new swing of public opinion, marketers and operations directors were jumping for joy at the opportunity to cut costs while simultaneously marketing their good deeds and collectively patting themselves on the back. Cutting down on the amount of plastic used in their products, implementing recycled goods, creating more energy efficient processes—you name it. But it soon became clear that while these quick fixes might win some short-term points in the mind of the consumer, no **green-washing** campaign can disguise your true purpose.

When the bottled water company FIJI® was on the verge of launching their new marketing strategy, they came up with the brilliant idea to market how eco-friendly their bottling process was. Unlike other water companies who purify old water and mass-produce it in industrialized factories, FIJI® taps their water directly from the natural aquifer in a clean and "green" process. Sounds like a great message, right? Wrong! In fact, this marketing campaign ended up haunting FIJI® for years. So, what went wrong?

FIJI's® marketing department didn't consider the massive carbon footprint that the company produced in transporting their product. The fact is, FIJI® is one of the only waters that is sourced in one hemisphere of the world and consumed in the other. The sheer amount of biodiesel needed to import the product was five times more damaging to the environment than the processes used by domestic bottling.

Shortly after launching their "green" campaign, the EPA and consumers alike criticized the brand for trying to appear to be something that it was not. They came off as a wolf dressed in sheepskin. The lesson here is that adopting a purpose-driven storyline just for the sake of marketing *will not work*. The public will cite you on your incongruities, and it will come back to bite you.

> **There is too much information in the marketplace now to use puffery as a viable tactic. You must actually live the purpose.**

8.1 Embracing the Opposite Side of Corporate Vanity

Around the same time as the FIJI® fiasco, a shoe company in America began to market a new idea for responsible consumerism. TOMS® shoes vowed to donate a pair of shoes to those in need for every pair that was purchased. Their brand purpose was to help the world walk more comfortably.

While the quality of the shoes produced by TOMS® was distinctly inferior to their larger competitors, these shoes gained massive appeal in the American marketplace because of the brand's generous purpose. Marketers and advertisers alike were scratching their heads at this phenomenon. Were people really purchasing an inferior product—and at a higher price—based solely on the brand's mission? Were consumers being *Sold On Purpose*? Yep!

While TOMS® initial advertising budget was very small, they successfully used the orientation effect to leverage the most important asset they had. You guessed it: purpose.

First-Movers

In this new purpose-driven economy, novelty is huge. The first mover brands have the highest probability of capitalizing on public perception. For instance, if a brand called "TIMS" came out to compete with TOMS® with a similar purpose, they would run the risk of looking like a copycat brand. Even if their brand purpose was authentic, the first movers in this market are the ones who stand to gain the most authentic perception of purpose. In fact, being the first one to a strong claim of purpose can solidify the ownership simply because you are the first one to put a flag in the sand. So before the world is off to the races, your brand needs to *claim its purpose*.

Here is a good example of someone who embraced honesty to earn the trust of consumers. In 2010, Domino's® was getting dominated by Pizza Hut®, Papa John's®, and all the other competitors. For years, they survived pretty much because their pizza was cheap. They were the underdog in the market. Then Domino's® came out with an ad campaign and told the world what the world already knew. They launched an "our pizza sucks" style ad campaign where they apologized for making bad pizza. They announced their intent to re-engineer all of their pizzas to be the best. People were surprised at Domino's® vulnerability. Big brands hadn't really ever done this before on TV.

When they did this, they embraced something that the marketplace loves: authenticity. For years, brands have been so self-serving and one-dimensional that when a company actually says something really authentic—particularly something that isn't 100 percent positive—people really listen. When Domino's® owned up to their poor-quality product, the consumer was suddenly laughing with them instead of at them. It elicited empathy from the audience. Not only did Domino's® promise to make their product better, but they also explained why: because they felt their consumers deserved more.

In the midst of this, Domino's® also sought to identify the barriers preventing them from being a good company. This resulted in a pothole campaign a few years later based on the concept of improving the roads their consumers drive on to pick up their pizza. So now, Domino's® is filling potholes in communities. What in the world does that have to do with pizza? Not much. But it has everything to do with the purpose-told story they are creating as a brand.

If the old purpose of Domino's® was to make money from selling pizza, their new purpose is making the best pizza and doing what's right for their communities. Other brands have since latched onto the anti-vanity marketing concept. They've come to realize that recommitting themselves to their consumers, in the form of owning up to their shortcomings, makes them appear more authentic.

As you can see, a purpose story doesn't have to be a big, world-changing mission. The only real prerequisite is that it is aimed at serving a higher purpose other than self.

Abandoning Corporate Vanity

Greek mythology introduced us to Narcissus, the most handsome hunter in all the world. Some versions of the story claim that the very sight of his beauty would paralyze his prey. One day, as he walked to the water's edge, he looked down at his reflection and fell in love with his own image. He stared back at himself in infatuation for days on end. He could not bring himself to leave his reflection to hunt or even take a drink of water. Narcissus, captivated by his own reflection in the water, withered away and perished.

This same vanity complex plagues brands who market themselves like Narcissus—so hopelessly in love with themselves that their own vanity will be the source of their downfall. Vanity is not inspiring, yet so many marketers use vanity as their main narrative.

One of the best things to understand about your audience is that they have an appetite for curiosity. One of the key ingredients in good storytelling is an uncertain outcome. When you give a viewer something they weren't expecting, they feel as if they have walked away with value. Domino's® dominated this in the pizza market. At the time, no one would have expected a commercial for a pizza restaurant to feature consumer testimonials claiming that their crust tasted like cardboard. This combination of violating expectations and abandoning corporate vanity proved to be a profitable strategy that ulti-mately helped them connect more with their consumers. While all the other pizza competitors patted themselves on the back for how great they were, little did they know they were becoming paralyzed by their own image.

You can't just yell and sell to your audience anymore. You must reward them with something they weren't expecting. Give them the honesty and authenticity they yearn for, even if it puts the brand in a vulnerable light. Most importantly, make your marketing for your consumers, not yourself, so you can avoid the same outcome exemplified in the story of Narcissus.

Chapter 9:

The Client is Always the Audience: Making Content for the Audience, Not the Brand

To some people, "marketing" is a dirty word. I guess I can't blame them. Marketers do have a way of bastardizing just about everything they touch. Don't forget: in the early days of the internet, people read their emails. Every single word, every single line, of every single email—they actually read them! Then marketers got involved and messed it all up. Pretty soon, our inboxes were saturated with e-blasted sales pitches and spam mail by the dozen. Nowadays, if it smells like a sale within the first line, I don't have the time to read the rest to even determine whether it's of any value. If I don't know the person and it just looks like a sales email, I delete it.

The spray-and-pray methods of sending out millions of messages just aren't effective anymore. Millennials are savvy consumers, so marketers need to find new ways to hook them good and hold them longer. This is no easy business. As marketers, the key thing we need to understand is our audiences' perspective. Is the content you made actually providing something meaningful and valuable to the viewer? Is it a story worth watching?

In this new age, content shouldn't be about product or even the brand. It should be about the consumer and the cause. This is the shift from a focus on content meant for transactional actions to content meant for transformational actions.

9.1 The Power of Branded Entertainment

There are millions of hours of content being produced daily, and meanwhile, the average production time spent per content piece is steadily decreasing. Anyone can now become famous on their own terms, any idea can become made known, and any product can have mass appeal if you can understand the methodology to **content virality**. For content creators, the chances of selling your indie documentary or low-budget film used to be one in a million. But now, Hulu®, Netflix®, HBO Go®, Amazon Prime®, and a ton of other providers are competing *for* content. This is one of the first times since the birth of the film industry that *there is more demand for content than there is supply*.

Prior to the internet, marketers controlled a lot of consumer behavior. If you wanted to watch a show, you could do that—at the expense of having to watch their ads. This was how brands communicated in the traditional mass media marketing model, and it gave them a lot of leeway. After all, when you're shoving something down someone's throat, it doesn't matter what it tastes like.

Now, in the digital age, people are choosing the flavors they like. The consumers control their interactions. In response, the most innovative brands are choosing to produce the kind of content their consumers enjoy. Lego® is making feature films. Dr. Pepper® is making a documentary. Red Bull® is making new action sports shows every week. These brands understand that the client is the audience.

The golden branded entertainment connection of content marketing occurs when the right content is in the right place at the right time for the right person. This is the home run of connections.

Branded Entertainment: Earn Your Wings

If you go to Red Bull's® website, you'll see that they barely even show their product. Instead, they cater custom content toward people who are interested in extreme sports.

Red Bull® has aligned itself with the values of these adrenaline-driven sports. They cater to extreme sports junkies, and their product actually comes *second* to their content. They create all kinds of content that cater precisely to their market, targeting the passion of their consumers.

By consistently producing content that aligns with their consumers' key values, Red Bull® has empowered their audience by making them feel connected and giving them content they want *on their terms*. To the viewer, this isn't just branded content, it's quality entertainment. All the while, the positive feelings and emotions that the viewers are experiencing while watching the content are being embedded into their subconscious as a positive learned association with the brand.

Over time, these repeated positive memories and interactions with the brand significantly increase the likelihood that viewers will consume their products. So the next time these consumers are in the grocery store and choosing between a

Red Bull® and a Monster Energy Drink®, chances are, the Red Bull® feels like the right choice.

Become a Partner

When you position yourself as a brand that empowers your audience—the mentor aiding the hero—you become a partner working with them instead of just a product or service provider.

In the old model, businesses and corporations were providers. In the new model, they are partners.

The idea of partnering with your audience is much more reciprocal than being a provider. You are now empowering the audience, and, in return, they feel obligated to empower you. They're giving some, and you're giving some—it's a two-way relationship.

Changing the message from providing to partnering allows the audience to understand that the relationship is interconnected. It's not codependent, it's inter-dependent. You need the consumer as much as they need your product, and that acknowledgment empowers them.

A quick additional note on content creation: Millennials expect this stuff for **free**.

I know that this may come off as an issue of entitlement or expecting something for nothing, but that's the price of admission to their hearts and minds. As their partner, your goal is not to score ROI every time they watch your content. You're working to build loyalty by constantly being a reflection of their worldview and the identity they wish to be.

Manufactured Authenticity and the Casino Floor

The expression of your purpose is essential, but expressing a false purpose in the digital age is brand suicide.

Some brands are interested in creating *manufactured authenticity*. This oxymoron is what so many brands try to do. It might work for a little while, but it just won't pay off in the long term. (Remember what happened to FIJI®?) The day is quickly approaching when consumers start shining a spotlight on *all* the shady tricks that have worked so well for years.

As an example, retailers have been under heavy criticism lately because a segment of consumers found out that companies were systematically affecting store temperatures and using spatial disorientation to increase sales. The news broke that some top retailers were lowering the temperatures in their stores by almost eight degrees to increase their winter wear sales, and it worked. But now that consumers have seen that they have been manipulated, their trust and lifetime value could be compromised.

Another technique that bubbled up to the surface recently was the method of **spatial disorientation** in big box retailers. A study found that subjects performed significantly worse at cognitive tasks after they had gone through a maze. It's just like a computer. If you overload the RAM, it can't work at optimal capability. Effective spatial disorientation influences your mind, giving you only a certain amount of bandwidth for cognitive responses.

IKEA® has been accused of reportedly assembling their store experiences based on this theory. Their stores are essentially enormous showrooms arranged in a maze. There's one entrance and one exit. They take you upstairs. They take you around turns, make you follow paths between couches and around living room sets. Then you go downstairs, where you start to feel a little claustrophobic, taking more twists and turns. By the time you get to the purchasing decision, you're so twisted and spun around by this maze that your cognitive processes are compromised. People will buy the ten things they didn't need … and forget the one thing they came for. They may get all the way to check-out before they remember. But what are they going to do? Retrace their steps all the way back through that maze? "Forget it. We'll just have to come back next weekend."

Casinos do the same thing, and they do it masterfully. A casino floor is the definition of old-school, yell-and-sell advertising. The machines are flashing with bright lights. There are no windows, so you can't even tell if it's day or night. And as far as the maze goes, if you've ever tried to get in or out of any hotel in Las Vegas, you will find that you *have* to walk through the casino to get to the exit.

These tactics may work, but it doesn't mean that they are good ideas. Do you think your consumers would appreciate it if they found out that one of your primary selling techniques was to intentionally compromise their cognitive abilities? To lull them into submission to buy a jacket because your store is freezing? Or run them through a maze to deliberately confuse the hell out of them? This is a liability to the trustworthiness of the brand short-term gain, but long-term loss.

Chapter 10:

Living Your Story – How to Show Your Values and Prove Your Purpose

Recently, there was a social experiment completed by NRG at the Miami International Airport that attempted to answer the question: does it matter to people where their energy is created?

Researchers set up a wall with four separate sections of phone-charging stations. Each section gave them choices in terms of the source of their energy; you could plug in to charge from energy produced by oil, by wind turbines, by solar energy, or by coal. After less than thirty minutes, a group of people were all plugged into wind and solar energy, and no one was using traditional fossil fuels. Faced with various alternatives, people did actually stop and consider their options. It was observed that people were making conscious choices about which port they plugged into. If all things are equal, I'll choose this one, because this is what I believe.

So, if all things equal, does it matter where your money goes? Does it feel a little bit better to know that by choosing

Airbnb® over a hotel chain, you just helped a fellow citizen out, rather than increasing Paris Hilton's net worth? If your answer is yes—even if your answer is maybe—this shows that brands can differentiate based on purpose.

The mindset of the consumer is becoming increasingly oriented toward considering complex social/environmental consequences in the buying decision. We see clear evidence of this in the fact that consumers are asking for things like all-organic foods, socially conscious manufacturing overseas, energy efficiency, chemically conscious processing, and environment-conscious packaging. People are thinking more about the whole, as opposed to the small part they interact with. That collective mindset is beginning to permeate the purchasing process, as well as the brand alignment process, which is why I chose to close this book with a chapter on the complexity of *how to show your values and prove your purpose*.

Brands today are selling lifestyles as opposed to products. It says something about the lifestyle of a person who owns an Apple® computer and drives a BMW®, as opposed to a person who rides a Harley Davidson®.

10.1 Public Opinion Matters

Studies have shown that social media users spend twice as long reading the comments of a post as they spend reading the post itself. What does this tell us? This demonstrates that in this hyper-connected environment we live in today, **public opinion is very important to individuals.** We care what other people think.

Today, instead of brands launching campaigns for consumers, consumers are influencing brand campaigns.

There used to be a much stronger polarity regarding gender, homosexuality, and other hot-button topics, but companies weren't expected to take stances on these issues. Now, if your brands take the unpopular side on a certain issue, you may find yourself in the minority—and the subject of public ire.

When a brand is not making a socially conscious effort to do things in the marketplace that align with public opinion, this could lead to a potential marketing misstep. One way or another, there will be consequences. The unfortunate reality is that brands can no longer remain neutral anymore.

A brand cannot be moral with the ability to act and stand still because to stand still is to choose indifference and indifference is the opposite of morals.

Purpose-Built Content Conquers All

Today, consumers trust one another more than they trust brands. They don't read the manufacturer description, but they do read the consumer reviews.

The book *Pendulum* by Roy H. Williams and Michael R. Drew theorizes that modern societies exist on an oscillating pendulum of cultural ideals. We are constantly shifting back and forth from a collective, more socially minded society to more individualistic ways of thinking. The 60s and 70s saw free love, anti-war, anti-establishment, and anti-corporate sentiments. The 80s ushered in a me-first era where making money was cool again. Instead of rebelling against the establishment, people wanted to find a profitable place within it, and corporations could do whatever they wanted, for the most part. This thinking persisted into the 90s. But now, we're swinging back again. *Saturation leads to critical mass, which ultimately leads to a reversal.* Today, the pendulum is swinging back toward a collective mindset.

In the same respect, I think we're moving toward a point where the oversaturation of media might cause the pendulum to swing back again. We see this exemplified in the recent "vintage" movement—the old and lame becoming new and cool again. I see people doing a lot of stuff with vinyl records and Polaroid® cameras. These analog equivalents to digital devices seem to have gained more appeal now that people have become inundated with digital.

It's not just the novelty of these things. The Millennials are so entrenched in our digital society that they see intrinsic value in the tangible, old stuff of the past. The movement to unplug is underway, and some brands like Vitamin Water®, who created a $100k unplug challenge that paid consumers to put their smart phone down for a year, are letting society know they agree with this sentiment.

Will this shift impact the story your brand should be telling? Maybe. That's for you to decide. Again, the point is to see not just where the consumer is but where they are going.

10.2 How to Differentiate Based on Purpose

What do you really sell?

Uber® doesn't sell transportation; they sell time and convenience with a click of a button. You're not calling a cab. You're not waiting or walking. You have moved from point A to point B.

Airbnb® doesn't sell rooms; they sell an experience. You could get a room from a hotel, but you won't get the same experience. You're bunking in a real person's house. Maybe they have a cool hot tub or some interesting art or an eclectic arrangement of things. You don't really know what you will get. They're selling adventure. When they know that, they can market it.

Nike® doesn't sell shoes; they sell identity. You want to be like Jordan? He wore these shoes. You want to be LeBron? He wears these shoes. The name Nike® is derived from the Greek goddess of victory. That's what they sell. An identity of victory. And they make that the theme in all of their branding. They understand, at a deeper level, what they're selling. I think the consumer understands that, too.

Red Bull®. Monster®. Apple®. Tesla®. These are all companies that understand that their true product is not their product. It's all subtext. I learned years ago that I don't sell videos, I sell emotion. That's what people are really coming to Diamond View to buy and once I understood my true product everything else clicked. Figure out what your true product is and this will aid in your purpose.

Do Good, Well

Today, we are an all-organic, energy-efficient, chemically conscious, tobacco-free, sustainably sourced, eco-friendly, inclusively diverse, gender-neutral society. The movement of movements is giving most brands motion sickness. But if you can understand one thing about all these movements, you can use them to your advantage:

> **The direction of all social movements is toward the perceived center of good.**

Those who are seeking a benevolent cause as their purpose will be greatly rewarded in this new-age marketplace.

If society's perspective of propriety is shaping behavior now and in the near future, can we predict new ideological shifts to come? Can we plot the social movements of the past to discover the potential movements of the future—predict the imminent swing of the pendulum? Can we use these insights to help build brand purpose(s) today that mature into social trends tomorrow? And can we organically position brands to be the leaders of their respective social movements?

Research shows that these movements are predicted to increase over the next ten to fifteen years thanks to the interconnection of social media and its tendency to expose our core values. As I mentioned previously, I believe there is a social movement on the near horizon that seeks to overcome the injustice of false media and the oppression of corporate propaganda on society. With the increasingly volatile social trends, I see traditional news and advertising becoming undesirable channels among the Millennial and Gen Z populations.

The Final Move

Now, as you stand at the crossroads of traditional advertising and a new paradigm of marketing, I urge you to take the path less traveled and market with meaning.

The age-old adage to "treat thy neighbor as thyself" should be your mantra as you progress. Constantly ask yourself, "Am I marketing to consumers in a way that I would like to be marketed to?"

As an imperative to your new marketing process, always *give value* instead of extracting it, because when we all begin to view marketing as the process of adding value to the world, marketing can become a powerful catalyst for good. Identify your current state of purpose and create an action plan to start transcending to the higher states.

There is a moment at the end of every book when you stare at the final page, and as the page stares back, you wait to see who makes the first move. Make the move! I've included a page for your to write down your purpose story at the end of this book. I must stress that your first move should be to clarify your purpose and to prioritize the passionate articulation of your purpose story that gives evidence of this statement.

Use the story archetypes in Chapter Five to structure your authentic story in a powerful way. Refine it over and over again until you distill it down to its most powerful form. This foundation gives insight to all actions and provides an understanding of complex decision-making. While it may seem at times that you are moving backward in order to move forward, you must *first sell yourself on your purpose before you can sell the world on your purpose*. I assure you, once you have this tangible understanding, it will be your greatest asset.

Thanks for taking the time to read the ideas brought forth in this book. I hope this has helped bring you further along in your quest for understanding marketing with purpose. I pray that, armed with this new information, you spread the message and inspire a new era of marketers to move toward purpose-driven marketing, and that your brand becomes a leader to empower others to find their calling.

One brand at a time, one story at a time, I look forward to a day when real meaning becomes the universal language, and the whole world is Sold on Purpose.

Brand Purpose Statement:

_____

_____

_____

_____

Brand Purpose Story:

_____

_____

_____

_____

_____

_____

_____

_____

_____

_____

_____

_____

_____

_____

_____

_____

_____

_____

_____

_____

Brand Purpose Statement:

_____

_____

_____

_____

Brand Purpose Story:

_____

_____

_____

_____

_____

_____

_____

_____

_____

_____

_____

_____

_____

_____

_____

_____

_____

Brand Purpose Statement:

_____

_____

_____

_____

Brand Purpose Story:

_____

_____

_____

_____

_____

_____

_____

_____

_____

_____

_____

_____

_____

_____

_____

_____

_____

_____

_____

_____

_____

Brand Purpose Statement:

_____

_____

_____

_____

Brand Purpose Story:

_____

_____

_____

_____

_____

_____

_____

_____

_____

_____

_____

_____

_____

_____

_____

_____

_____

About the Author

Tim Moore is a three-time Emmy award-winning director and CEO of Diamond View, a video agency headquartered in Florida. As a curiously driven entrepreneur, Tim has become a leading expert in purpose-driven marketing over the last 10 years and has developed emotionally compelling campaigns for brands all around the world. He is also the founder of the Tampa Foundation, a 501(c)(3) non-profit focused on inspiring communities through positive public messaging.

Tim is also currently in production of a patent pending technology called DSR, Dynamic Scene Replacement, that offers advertisers the ability to increase the emotional effectiveness of advertising by autonomously replacing scenes based on viewer affinity data.

For more information on the author and ideas brought forth in this book visit SoldOnPurpose.com

Glossary

- **Ad Hominem Advertising** - Advertising focused on emotional appeal by attacking the opposition's character as opposed to logical appeal.

- **Audience Fragmentation** - The separation of audience groups from the mass audience phenomenon due to specialized, personalized content created as a result of new media applications.

- **Autonomous Sensory Meridian Response (ASMR)** - An experience characterized by a static-like tingling sensation on the skin that typically begins at the scalp and moves down the back of the neck and upper spine.

- **Brand Ambassadors** - A person who is either hired by an organization or volunteers to represent a brand in a positive light and by doing so help to increase brand awareness and sales.

- **Brand Loyalty** - The tendency of some consumers to continue buying the same brand of goods over and over again rather than competing brands.

- **Brand Storytelling** - The use of narrative storytelling in marketing to connect a brand to its consumers, often with a heavy focus on values and purpose rather than product features or benefits.

- **Branded Entertainment** - A form of branded content that is often used as disguised marketing to give prospective consumers value while allowing brands to position themselves in the content.

- **Call to Belief** - A new form of the "Call to Action."

- **Cause Marketing** - A type of corporate social responsibility in which a company's promotional campaign has the dual purpose of increasing profitability while bettering society.

- **Cause Positioning** - The positioning of both a brand and a cause in a way that influences the consumer to perceive the relationship of the brand and cause with a certain determined effect (often characterized by positioning the brand as the hero to the cause).

- **Clarity of Purpose** - The definiteness of understanding an individual or organizations meaning for existence and role in the world.

- **Classical Conditioning** - The learning process in which two stimuli are linked together to produce a new learned response in a person or animal.

- **Collective Opinion** - The synchronistic opinion of a large population

- **Conscious Consumer** - A consumer that uses corporate responsibility as a deciding factor in the purchasing decision of a product or service.

- **Content Marketing** - A form of marketing focused on creating, publishing, and distributing content for a targeted audience.

- **Content Virality** - The exponential metric an article, an image or a video that spreads rapidly online through website links and social sharing and often times shared in peer to peer networks online.

- **Corporate Euthanasia -** The bankruptcy of a corporation a result of consumers choosing to boycott their brand or products, often times as a deliberate result of dollar voting.

- **Corporate Social Responsibility (CSR) -** The self-regulating business model that helps a company be socially and environmentally accountable — to itself, its stakeholders, and the public.

- **Diminishing Marginal Utility -** An effect, often found in economics, where the increase in quantity yields a decrease in utility.

- **Dollar Voting -** The deliberate support or boycott of certain brands or companies based on their core values or beliefs.

- **Dual Consumption of media (multi-screen content consumption) -** Using two, or more, connected devices at once.

- **Emotional Sight Reading -** The covert emotional association of a product or service as portrayed in an advertisement.

- **Empowerment Marketing -** A marketing style in which the messaging is meant to empower the consumer. It is often times created without the end goal of getting a short term transaction sale or extracting value from the consumer, but rather aimed at brand loyalty and long term affinity from the consumer to the brand.

- **Founder's Passion Story -** A purpose story archetype that uses a company's founding passion as the motivator and purpose to the company's creation.

- **Frisson -** Frisson is a quick onset of piloerections that move across different sections of the body like the arms or legs.

- **Green-Washing** - A manipulative marketing technique in which green PR or green marketing is deceptively used to promote the perception that an organization's products, aims or policies are environmentally friendly.

- **Hero's Journey** - A purpose story archetype that is modeled of Joseph Campbell's mono-myth structure where a hero character is given a gift by a mentor character to heal a broken world.

- **Horizontal Marketing** - A form of marketing that leverages consumers opinions to remarket to their peers about particular products or services. (ex. Consumer Reviews, Product Opinions on Social Media, etc.)

- **Horizontal Marketplace** - A peer to peer marketplace in which a consumer influence other consumers opinions on products or services.

- **Idealistic Purpose** - When individuals use their purpose toward the greater good, often characterized by depleting their resources for the betterment of others and act counterintuitive to accumulation and survival.

- **Inadequacy Marketing** - An old age marketing model that manipulates viewers by preying on their insecurities.

- **Inspirational Interest Segmentation** - Creating strategic content based on known stakeholder interests to increase engagement.

- **Interruptive Advertising** -The interruptive promotion of a product through advertising, promotions, public relations or sales in the middle of an entertainment media. It is often considered an unflattering marketing tactic whereby companies interrupt their consumers entertainment experience.

- **Latent Learning** - Knowledge that only becomes clear when a person has an incentive to display it.

- **Leading Edge** - A person who starts using a product or technology as soon as it becomes available.

- **Learned Association** - Any learning process in which a new response becomes associated with a particular stimulus.

- **Manufactured Associations** - Artificially associated feelings or beliefs to an idea or product created deliberately by an organization or brand.

- **Manufactured Authenticity** - The artificial creation of perceivably genuine storylines often made to position a brand or company in a positive light toward a social cause or environmental outcome.

- **Mirror Story** - A purpose story archetype that uses the consumer experience as a framework for describing the brands purpose meant to mirror the life experience of the viewer and relate on a deeper level.

- **Neuro-Linguistic Programming** - An approach to communication, personal development, and psychotherapy created by Richard Bandler and John Grinder in California in the 1970s that aims to influence behavior and outcomes based on particular word patterns and choice of speech.

- **Orientation Effect** - An effect in marketing where the consumers belief system toward a value and the brands belief system toward that value allow both the brand and consumer to create the optimum connection. This ultimately offers leverage to the brand to reasonably expand that belief system.

- **Over The Top (OTT)** - A term used to refer to content providers that distribute streaming media as a standalone product directly to viewers over the internet.

- **Participation Age** - A modern age predicted by Phillip Kotler in his book Marketing 3.0, where consumers participate in marketing activities that where previously exclusive to brands (examples include Wikipedia, Micro-Blogging, Social Media, etc.).

- **Peer Validation** - A marketing system that leverages opinions of like peers to artificially increase the value or demand for a product or service.

- **Piloerection** - A bristling of hairs due to the involuntary contraction of small muscles at the base of hair follicles that occurs as a reflective response of the sympathetic nervous system, especially to cold, shock or fright. Often referred to as "Goosebumps" in common language.

- **Positive Cultural Association** - The association of positive feelings or beliefs by peers or cultural groups toward certain products or services.

- **Psuedo-Stories** -The manipulation of stories to create the perception of artificial outcomes often created to positively position the storyteller and negatively position their opponent. These type of stories often omit critical details of the real story which lead them to be false.

- **Public Relations** - The practice of deliberately managing the spread of information between an individualu, or an organization and the public.

- **Purpose Conundrum** - A complexity of perspective in which individuals or companies fail to discover their purpose because of the universal physical limitations of their own observations.

- **Purpose Economy** - An economy in which goods and services are traded and sold based on the greater purpose of the organizations that produce them often leading to benefits in the larger ecosystem by trickle down benefits.

- **Purpose Story** - A story used to describe the reason for an individual or organization's existence, often used to describe higher forms of values and goals.

- **Purposive Behaviorism** - A branch of psychology that combines the objective study of behavior while also considering the purpose or goal of behavior.

- **Social Confirmation** - A marketing system that leverages the opinions of certain social groups to artificially increase the value or demand for a product or service.

- **Social Influence** - A marketing system that influences the opinion of buyers by marketing the perceived opinion of the public to artificially increase the value or demand for a product or service.

- **Spacial Disorientation** - A phenomenon in which human cognition is impared by the overstimulation of complex spaces.

- **Story Laundering** - The act of using similar stories of the past to create new stories.

- **Subliminal Command Clause** - A covert linguistic command that is used to influence a consumer toward a particular behavior.

- **Transformative Purpose** - The final state of purpose in which positive transformation occurs in the ecosystem making the individual or organization a necessary component of that ecosystem.

- **Unconditioned Response** - An unlearned response that occurs naturally in reaction to the unconditioned stimulus.

- **Vertical Advertising** - A traditional advertising model in which brands and consumers are oriented in a vertical fashion often characterized by communication separation where brands communicate to consumers but consumers cannot communicate easily back to brands.

CPSIA information can be obtained
at www.ICGtesting.com
Printed in the USA
BVHW081427290719
554568BV00025B/2359/P